The Monday Morning Fix

Your Weekly Cup of Inspiration

Tony Henry

The Monday Morning Fix

Disclaimer

The information contained in this book is for general information purposes only. The information is provided by Tony Henry and while we endeavour to keep the information up to date and correct, we make no representations or warranties of any kind, express or implied, about the completeness, accuracy, reliability, suitability or availability with respect to this publication or the information, products, services, or related graphics contained in this publication for any purpose. Any reliance you place on such information is therefore strictly at your own risk.

In no event will we be liable for any loss or damage including without limitation, indirect or consequential loss or damage, or any loss or damage whatsoever arising from loss of data or profits arising out of, or in connection with, the use of this publication.

Through this publication you are able to link to other resources and contacts which are not under the control of Tony Henry. We have no control over the nature, content and availability of those responsible for their management, operation or function. The inclusion of any links does not necessarily imply a recommendation or endorse the views expressed within them.

At the time of writing, every effort was made to keep the information in this publication current. However, Tony Henry takes no responsibility for, and will not be liable for, information being out of date or unavailable due to technical or any other issue beyond our control.

Contact Tony Henry at:
Info.elevation7@gmail.com

Copyright Year: April 2018, First edition

Copyright Notice: Published by Tony Henry. All rights reserved. No part of this book may be reproduced in any form or by any means whatsoever, unless where permission is granted by Tony Henry.

Results in this copyright notice:

© 2018 Tony Henry. All rights reserved

ISBN: 978-1-909389-27-4

Tony Henry

The Monday Morning Fix

Your Weekly Cup of Inspiration

Dedication

To my dear parents George and Margaret Henry who sadly are no longer with us R.I.P. George the king of common sense and Margaret the Queen of delayed gratification. My Role Models and my inspiration. Both came from very humble beginnings, both leaving a legacy larger than life. They had a dream of retiring back home to St Lucia. They managed to build their dream home, however they both paid a substantial price through the process and sadly never got to enjoy the fruits of their labour. My children Dean, Natasha, Nathan and Malik, a constant reminder that giving up was not an option. I thank you all for the lessons in living and pray that by God's grace I can continue in the footsteps of my father George Henry and be an inspiration to you all. My

grandchildren Junior, Alayah, Ayahna and Amayah for being the blessings that you are.

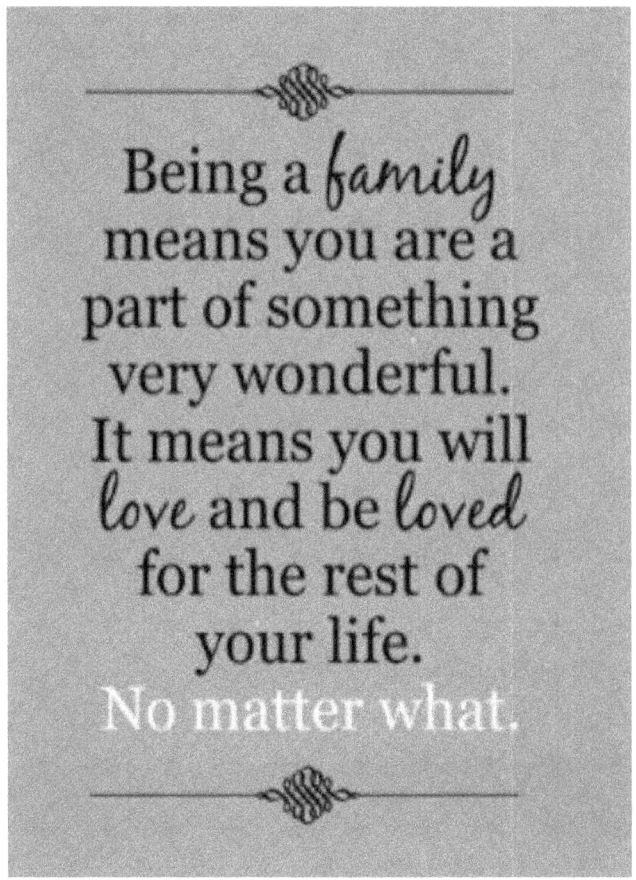

Contents

Acknowledgements		9
Foreword		12
About the Author – Tony Henry		14
Preface		16
Introduction		19
1.	Overcoming The Fear Of Success	22
2.	Resentment And The Blame Game	27
3.	Quitting The Blame Game	33
4.	What To Do When You Don't Know What To Do	39
5.	Actions Speak Louder Than Words	44
6.	Reclaim The Adult In You	48
7.	Know Who You Are, Know Yourself	53
8.	You Have Got to WORK At It!!!	58
9.	Perception vs Reality	63
10.	Time Out To Love Self	68
11.	Don't Stay Stuck	73
12.	Change: Mind, Body And Spirit	79
13.	Control Or Controlled	83
14.	Money! Money! Money!	88
15.	The Essence Of Self	92
16.	Withholding Your Feelings	97
17.	What Type Are You?	102

18.	Failure To Thrive (FTT)	106
19.	Feel The Fear And Do It Anyway	110
20.	Attitude	115
21.	Change Your Password, Change Your Life	119
22.	We Are Like Pencils	125
23.	The Rule of ONE	129
24.	Work To Live Or Live To Work	134
25.	Time Is the Master	138
26.	Black Or White	142
27.	Life Is Answering Your Requests	146
28.	Time	151
29.	The Hidden Gemstone	156
30	Passion Into Profit	160
31.	Stay Sharp	166
32	Mistakes Or (Lessons in Living)	171
33.	Seventy Percent	175
34.	Miracles Happen	179
35.	Failure Is Inevitable	184
36.	The Grass Isn't Greener	188
37.	The Good You Do, Comes Back To You	192
38.	Mind Over Matter	197
39.	Love…I Am Enough	201
40.	It's Not Over Till It's Over	205
41.	Echo	210

42.	Tapping Into Your Power	214
43.	Finish The Year Strong	218
44.	What Do You Make?	223
45.	Three Types Of People	227
46.	Making Sense Out Of Modern Day Nonsense	231
47.	Your Health Is Your Wealth	236
48.	The Giving Tree	242
49.	Where Will You Be Five Years From Today?	248
50.	Unique Different But Equal	253
51.	Self-Awareness	257
52.	The Value Of Life	262
Endorsements		267

Acknowledgements

Chris Day of Filament Books, for taking the time out to interview me, flushing out the untapped potential of not only *The Monday Morning Fix* but also my story and why I should seriously consider making it my second book.

Paul Crooks, for those timely interruptions and progress report check ins.

Shabazz Shillingford, my brother from another Mother. A big thank you for your wealth of knowledge both book and non-book related. Our conversations always leave me inspired.

To my fellow role model and friend - DD Armstrong - for supporting and encouraging me during the birthing stage of this book.

To my long-standing school mate and friend - Simon Borrows - for allowing me to be part of the process of his book which reinforced my belief in my own ability to produce my own.

Michael Bradford, for challenging me to start the writing process, timely advice short, sharp and sweet.

Wilton Hansel, for always believing in my ability to write and the timely words of encouragement when things seem to be going astray.

June Lawrence, for your no-nonsense approach, when it came to narrowing down the 52 chapters.

Nickayala Ramsey and Joseph Hanlon, for taking the time to start the initial editing process and giving me a wake call of the work to come.

Kwame MA McPherson and the Baobab Tree Publishing team for supporting me in making this dream become a reality.

Iyanla Vanzant for your book Until Today, which shone a light on what is possible. Allowing me to discover more of myself and the power of devotions.

Derek Walcott, 1992 St Lucian Noble Prize winner in Literature, an awesome inspiration for what is possible.

My partner and best friend Janice Tape, for all your support, encouragement, hard work, awesome energy and unconditional love.

Last but no means least, I would like to thank all my family, friends, teachers, mentors, role models, work associates and business partners for their continued contributions to my personal development.

Foreword

I first met Tony at one of my life transformation seminars in London over a decade ago and it fills my heart with joy to see where he has come from, to where he is heading. He was one of the few that stayed close to the fire and was committed to personal growth and making a difference.

Over the years we became familiar and eventually friends. I remember when he first started sending me his Monday Elevation messages, I enjoyed the short and sweet format and knew he was onto something. In our journey of friendship, Tony has weathered the storms and his consistency demonstrates his commitment and genuine passion to make a difference. He has grown tremendously in this time and his unique ability to communicate in a way that connects, is the power of his work. His vast experience and exposure in working with schools, prisons and organisations, brings life into his words.

When Tony first told me about his book journey, I got so excited.

So many people will gain from his messages and more importantly, the structured learning approach, weekly lessons combined with weekly actions to help the reader implement what has been learnt. One of the biggest struggles of knowledgeable people is that they struggle to transfer what they know into their lives.

If you are on the path of self-awareness and personal transformation, then this is a great workbook that will accelerate your journey. Writing a book is a huge accomplishment and for this I applaud you – Tony – I am so proud of you.

Much Love and Success Always my friend.

"Your Personal Growth & Awareness is the biggest gift you can give back to the world"

Kalpesh Patel

Trained over 500,000 Entrepreneurs and Leaders
Top 60 International Speakers List
Top 50 Direct Sales Leaders Worldwide
International Podcast, TV, Radio, News & Web Interviews & Author
#TheKalpeshPatel & www.TheKalpeshPatel.com
Co-Founder of www.WorldTransformationOrg.com #WTD

About The Author – Tony Henry

When Tony Henry aka The Liftdoctor came by this name, it was no accident. *The Monday Morning Fix* illustrates Tony's passion for supporting his audience to realise their dreams and fulfil their potential. Through weekly inspirational stories and illustrations, *The Monday Morning Fix* is designed to disrupt the drudgery of the 9-5.

Whether you come into contact with Tony as an Author, a Coach, Role Model, Mentor or Speaker, you are going to walk away inspired, motivated along with a can-do mentality. In addition, his energy and charisma are awe-inspiring and definitely come across in his work.

To ensure he provides what he says he will, Tony:

- Has a Certificate in Training with Mental Health Speciality
- A Certificate as a Motivational Map Practitioner
- A Certificate as a Master Coach

In addition, Tony has a BA – Balanced Achiever, LLB - Living Life Beautifully, a PHD - Past Having Doubt and is currently studying for his MBA - Mega Bank Account!

Tony Henry

A father of four and a grandfather of four, Tony describes himself as the modern-day Benjamin Button.

> *"Imagination is everything, it's the preview of life's coming attractions"*
> **Albert Einstein**

> *"When you change the way you look at things; the things you look at change"*
> **Wayne Dyer**

Preface

Having played around with writing for many years, my transition came from two sources, my son Malik who has had his work published twice, well done son. And a chance encounter with a stranger (Michael Bradford), who I had the pleasure of meeting whilst on a weekend training. It started with Michael coming up to me out of the blue on the Friday and informing me there was a book in me and then just as casually, disappearing into the crowd.

Reappearing on the Sunday, he informed me that there were books in me however, my first task was to start writing, not get hung up on the how, book titles or chapters. I was to find a cause and just start writing since the rest would take care of itself.

Years down the road I found my cause, I read an article which posed the question: *"What is the most likely day of the week to have a heart attack?"* Answer Monday. Why? Because Friday was pay day and the start of the weekend and for the majority of people, the start of something good. Saturday reinforced the fact that the weekend had begun and by Sunday, after lunch or dinner, the dreaded thought of returning to the J.O.B (Just Over Broke) would begin to bring many people down with a bump. Hey, presto I had found my cause!

What if I could write an article that encouraged, inspired, motivated or just simply changed the mood of despair to one of gratitude and hope. Taking a half-empty cup and transforming it into a half-full cup full of encouragement, inspiration, positivity and light. Well my friends there you have it, that is how *The Monday Morning Fix* (MMF) was birthed.

> You cannot control what happens to you, but you can control your attitude toward what happens to you, and in that, you will be mastering change rather than allowing it to master you.
>
> Brian Tracy, American Author

What would I like you take away from this book?

A message of **H.O.P.E (Having Only Positive Expectations)**, a reduction in **F.E.A.R (False Evidence Appearing Real)**, a sprinkle of **F.A.I.T.H (Full Acceptance in Trust and Hope)** and a splash of **F.O.C.U.S (Follow One Course Until Successful)**.

Embracing and understanding that bad things happen to good people, however coming to comprehend that within all of us is the ability to withstand adversity, to overcome and to thrive.

Introduction

Having developed a thirst for personal development, I felt an urge to introduce my own brand of motivation in the form of weekly inspirational tips, parables and lessons, designed to disrupt the perception of an overwhelming life. And by introducing these thought-provoking life lessons allowing you to reflect, rethink and create a new mindset. **Knowing that you need to improve your life takes insight and actually taking the necessary steps to make it happen, takes even more courage, focus and determination.**

With over half of all UK employees unhappy at work and the population at large disillusioned, it was unsurprising that Mondays have been cited as the most likely day of the week for someone to have a heart attack. Putting that into perspective, the average employee cannot wait for Friday. This theory was even backed by the London School of Business and Finance and written about in The Telegraph (Source: *It's official: most people are miserable at work*, The Telegraph, Wednesday 14th August 2019. www.telegraph.co.uk/). Whether that be because it was payday, start of the weekend or just time off work, it was sad to see how quickly that euphoria would come crashing down. As in under 48 hours when consuming Sunday lunch or dinner that thought of returning to work on Monday could descend like a plague from hell, wiping out any trace of the weekend's enjoyment.

How To Use This Book

The Monday Morning Fix is broken down into 52 chapters, one for each week of the year. Each week introducing a new topic to challenge your view on the subject matter and hopefully stimulate a conversation within yourself, giving you the opportunity to change the way you look at things. As the saying goes: *'When you change the way you look at things, the things you look at change.'*

The Reflection: It is for you - the reader - to identify what resonates with you and write it down. Since writing it down is where the magic happens. Create a clear, concise mental image of what stood out for you. Remembering it is never too late to set another goal or dream a new dream.

The Action Steps: Created for you to anchor down the whole experience. Write down what you believe to be necessary, to get what you say you want. Remembering what you focus on with your thoughts and feelings is what you attract.

The Affirmation: This is all about you and what you have taken from *The Monday Morning Fix*. Its purpose is designed for you to create a positive statement to make you feel clear, energetic and active. Putting you in a better position to transform your inner and outer worlds. When you say it, think it or hear it, it becomes your new reality. The simplest way to start your affirmation is to begin with an *"I am"* statement that describes what you want to have or experience.

1. Overcoming The Fear Of Success

"The greatest mistake you can make in life is to continually fear you will make one." - Elbert Hubbard

So, you say you want to be successful. REALLY? Let us examine for a moment some of the actions and attitude that might hold you back from being successful, and then gain a deeper insight as to where the fear might be coming from. For someone who's yet to experience true success, achieving the ultimate goal, there is a point when entering into the unknown, coming out of one's comfort zone and performing on a higher level mentally, physically, spiritually and emotionally that the fear of the unknown will kick in. When this happens, you may want to share your ideas, vision or dreams with those close to you like your friends and family. To your dismay the responses you receive may not always be filled with enthusiasm or encouragement. You might be told things like, *"People like us do not have access to those type of opportunities"*,

> The key to success is to focus our Conscious mind on things we desire not things we fear

"Who do you think you are kidding?", "Why would you want to give up the security of your day job?" or *"That sounds too risky."* The list goes on.

Having had your bubble burst you are now faced with more questions, *was it a mistake to share your thoughts? Do you believe that it is alright for the others but not for you? Are you afraid that when you start something you are going to fail?* Remember, *"**What you focus on the most, is what you attract.**"* Maybe there are a few limiting beliefs from past experiences which rear their ugly head that your mistakes will be repeated now and in the future, causing you to question whether or not you are able to succeed.

Mistake vs Challenge

Now, let us replace the word 'mistake' with the word *"challenge"*, as you know words have power. Committing to taking on more challenges will give you a mountain of experience from which will spring knowledge, allowing you to do incredible things. Stretch yourself at least once a day by taking yourself out of your comfort zone, challenging yourself to experience something new, e.g. volunteer to take on a new role at work. Allow the experience to wash over you, taking the learning from it and creating your own success library by documenting each and every one of your achievements.

Live in balance as success is not a destination it is a journey, and it is important that you take each step feeling grounded and balanced.

> *In order to succeed Your desire for success Should be greater than Your fear of failure*

Having a Vision

Achieving lasting change, and getting what you **really** want in life, takes a sustained vision of the future. That vision serves not just as an ongoing source of motivation, it also helps you to identify and tackle the obstacles that have held you back until now. Forgiving yourself when you fall short of the mark is a bitter but beneficial pill, which allows you to move on and not act out your failure over and over again. All fears of success would go away if you take your power back and follow through with your God-given talents and skills.

> "Our deepest fear is not that we are inadequate. Our deepest fear is that we are powerful beyond measure"
> **Nelson Mandela**

Tony Henry

Let Your Light Shine….

Reflection:

_____
_____
_____
_____
_____
_____
_____
_____
_____
_____
_____
_____

Action

1.

2.

3.

Tony Henry

Positive Affirmation to Self

2. Resentment And The Blame Game

"Resentment is anger with oneself, misdirected at someone else through the lens of victimhood"
Melissa Dinwiddie

- How does it make you feel reading the above statement?
- What questions run through your mind?
- Have you had an aha! moment or are you fueled by something else?

Many of us go through life without setting boundaries, falling in and out of relationships, jobs and situations never taking stock as to why we felt resentment to others for our lack of taking responsibility for ourselves and actions. *Is it by accident that we attract certain people and continue to find ourselves in the same situations over and over again?* No.

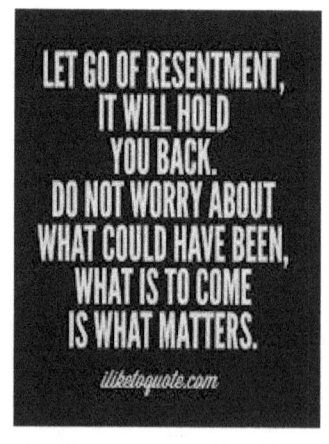

When you are trained to be a people-pleaser, setting clear limits is hard. It is easier to just go with the flow, and then get resentful and blame anybody or anything for not making a decision, allowing others to make decisions for you. Playing the victim does not lead to happiness or empowerment. Once you can acknowledge and understand that this is what you are doing, *"**playing the victim**,"* you need to take stock, regroup and determine to yourself that it is time for change.

Understand that resentment does not serve any useful purpose, understand where your anger is coming from and know that by setting clearer, stronger boundaries, you can release the resentment and work on making the changes you need for yourself.

> *"How you do some things is how you do everything."*
> **T Harv Eker**

Taking Responsibility

Taking responsibility for yourself extends to every area of your life, learning to set boundaries and communicate them is an essential tool for anyone looking for a happy life. Have you ever been in a situation where you have made a decision to do something, like start exercising or lose weight, got all excited only to find yourself allowing work and your environment to dictate your time and prevent you from starting? Then feeling resentful, falling into the blame game about how you could not find the time and if you only had the support of your partner or friend that you would have stood a better chance of success.

Ask yourself these questions:

- *Who was it that wanted to lose weight or exercise?*
- *How did you communicate the fact that you would like to enlist the support of your partner or friend?*
- *Who is accountable for you achieving your goal?*
- *Are you prepared to do what it takes to achieve your goal?*

> Forgiveness is the key that unlocks the door of resentment and the handcuffs of hatred. It is a power that breaks the chains of bitterness and the shackles of selfishness.
>
> Corrie Ten Boom
> meetville.com

You are the one who chose to stay at work, watch TV, snooze an extra hour in bed or go out with friends, instead of going to the gym or that weight loss class. The responsibility is yours and yours alone, any anger directed elsewhere is a pointless waste of time and energy. Your life is a reflection of where you are at any given point in time. Everything that is coming at you from out there, is coming to show you where work is needed. There is no point playing the blame game for what is going on with and around you. You are missing a divine opportunity to examine what is really going on within you. Learning to accept the apology you never got and forgiving yourself for allowing the mistakes of the past to impact your present, is important. Forgiving all those who have caused you harm knowingly or not, for we are all *"work in progress"* and so none of us are perfect. It would be foolhardy to hold resentment against a loved one, friend or boss who inadvertently caused you pain that does not make their actions right, however, it reinforces the fact that we are imperfect beings.

There are times when resentment sets in and you may believe that the only way forward is revenge. It is at this pivotal moment that you are to take stock and realise that forgiveness is the key. Some of you may believe that by forgiving you are letting the other person off the hook, truth be known, by not forgiving you have kept yourself hooked!

"Tomorrow belongs to the people who prepare for it today."
African Proverb

Reflection:

Action

1.
2.
3.

Positive Affirmation to Self

3. Quitting The Blame Game

It would appear that we are increasingly buying into a blame-oriented culture. *"It's the school's fault why my child lacks manners"*, *"If my boss would just invest more money into my training"*, any excuse. Today our misfortunes are deemed to be somebody else's fault. *"I'm this way because of them", "They did it to me", "Woulda, coulda shoulda"* the list goes on. The funny thing is, it didn't begin with us. It goes all the way back to Adam in the Garden of Eden when he told God *"The woman...You gave...me, she gave me of the tree, and I ate."* (Genesis 3:12 NKJV).

> it is not only for what we do that we are held responsible, but also for what we do not do.
> ~ Moliere

It is in Our DNA!

We say the breakdown in our marriage was our partner's fault, we drink too much because somebody drives us to it, or we are unwell because of the fast-food industry. Let's sue them! Shifting responsibility may alleviate momentary guilt but it is a deadly game with no winners.

The blame came naturally to Adam and Eve, the father and mother of the human race. After all, who could fault them? God did! Their blame was a result of how sin had changed them. Their relationship to themselves, each other, their environment, and even God, was radically changed by their irresponsibility and because of their reluctance to be accountable. They were evicted from paradise into the rat race that we know so well today, what a price to pay.

The Modern Day Adam and Eve

What does it take for the modern-day Adam and Eve to live a life of Accountability, Responsibility and Consistency, reaping the benefits of what life has to offer? Having been blessed with choice here are some good reasons why we should quit the blame game:

It makes you miserable. You say, *"But they hurt me."* Yes, and by harbouring resentment you are hurting yourself over and over. The Bible says, *"...Keep a sharp eye out for weeds of bitter discontent. A thistle or two gone to seed can ruin a whole garden in no time..."* (Hebrews 12:14-15 TM). Before you know it, your entire outlook gets distorted.

It makes you a victim. When you make someone else responsible for your circumstances, you put the power to change things in their hands. That means nothing will change unless they decide to change it. You make them master of your fate. Only by accepting personal responsibility can you retain the power to change your circumstances.

It creates enemies, the person you are blaming will ignore you, people around you will soon get tired of hearing your victim story and start to distance themselves from you. Your root of bitterness will spread, causing many to be infected by your virus, blaming rubs off and the more you do the more addictive it becomes, to the point where it is easier for you to complain rather than resolve your problems and issues.

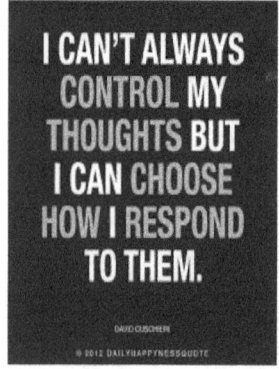

Stopping the Blame Game

Blaming sabotages forgiveness, you cannot forgive someone while you are judging and resenting them. Take a moment to reflect on how much time and energy you have squandered pointing the finger of blame as opposed to accepting responsibility for yourself, your actions and your choices.

Remember what enters your mind repeatedly first occupies your mind, and then eventually shapes your perception and reality. Your mind will absorb and ultimately reflect whatever it is repeatedly exposed to, harbouring resentment, anger and bitterness can only serve to harm you. Solution...release all attachment to the negative emotions of the past and make a commitment to experience love, joy, peace, forbearance, kindness, goodness, faithfulness, gentleness and self-control inviting balance back into your Life, Mind, Body and Spirit.

The happiest people do not have the best of everything; they make the best of everything.

Reflection:

_____
_____
_____
_____
_____
_____
_____
_____
_____
_____
_____
_____

Action

1.

2.

3.

Positive Affirmation to Self

4. What To Do When You Don't Know What To Do

With all that is currently taking place in society right now, there are many who are stuck as to what to do. Whether it is a decision around a relationship, job, career change or simply voting, the list for some appears endless. Trust in the process of life, resist the temptation for a quick fix. Life has shown all of us that a quick fix today will cost double tomorrow. For instance, you go with the cheapest quote to do a job only to have the same job carried out over again by more qualified person at a greater expense.

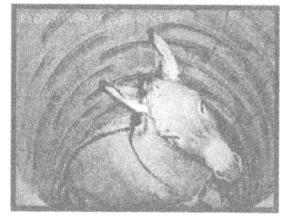

One day a farmer's donkey fell into a well. The animal cried piteously for hours as the farmer tried to figure out what to do. Finally, he decided the animal was old, and the well needed to be covered up anyway, it just was not worth retrieving the donkey. He invited all his neighbours to come over and help him. They all grabbed a shovel and began to shovel dirt into the well. At first, the donkey realised what was happening and cried horribly. Then, to everyone's amazement he quieted down.

A few shovel loads later, the farmer final looked down the well. He was astonished at what he saw. With each shovel of dirt that hit his back, the donkey was doing something amazing. He would shake it off and take a step up.

As the farmer's neighbours continued to shovel dirt on top of the animal, he would shake it off and take a step up. Pretty soon, everyone was amazed as the donkey stepped up over the edge of the well and happily trotted off.

MORAL OF THE STORY:

Life is going to shovel dirt on you, all kinds of dirt. The trick to getting out of the well is to shake it off and take a step up. Each of our troubles is a steppingstone. We can get out of the deepest wells just by not stopping, never giving up! Shake it off and take one step up at a time.

Remember these five simple rules to be happy:

1. Free your heart from hatred - Forgive.
2. Free your mind from worries – Might never happen.
3. Live simply and appreciate what you have.
4. Give more.
5. Expect less from people but more from yourself.

A set back is a set up for a comeback.

Reflection:

_____

_____

_____

_____

_____

_____

_____

_____

_____

_____

_____

_____

Action

1.

2.

3.

Positive Affirmation to Self

5. Actions Speak Louder Than Words
Who Do They Say You Are?

The light turned yellow just in front of him. He did the right thing, stopping at the crossing, even though he could have beaten the red light by accelerating through the intersection. The tailgating woman was furious and honked her horn, screaming in frustration, as she missed her chance to get through the intersection, dropping her cell phone and makeup. As she was still in mid rant, she heard a tap on her window and looked up into the face of a very serious-looking policeman. The officer ordered her to exit her car with her hands up. He took her to the police station where she was searched, fingerprinted, photographed, and placed in a holding cell.

After a couple of hours, a policeman approached the cell and opened the door. She was escorted back to the booking desk where the arresting officer was waiting with her personal effects.

He said, *"I am very sorry for this mistake. You see, I pulled up behind your car while you were blowing your horn, making rude gestures and verbally cursing like there was no tomorrow. I noticed the 'What Would Jesus Do?' bumper sticker, the 'Choose Life' license plate holder, the 'Follow Me to Sunday-School' bumper sticker, and the chrome-plated Christian fish emblem on the trunk, so naturally...I assumed you had stolen the car."*

Moral of the story

Practice what you preach, often people cannot hear you because of what you are doing, have faith in the process of life and adopt the mindset of a lifelong learner.

How you do anything, is how you do everything.

Reflection:

_____
_____
_____
_____
_____
_____
_____
_____
_____
_____
_____
_____

Action

1.

2.

3.

Positive Affirmation to Self

6. Reclaim The Adult In You

When as a child you were confronted with a challenge or felt fearful, did not get your own way. When you felt you were not heard, what was your response? Did you pout, stomp your feet, throw a temper tantrum or slam a door. When was the last time you slammed a door? Threw a temper tantrum? You an able bodied competent adult regressing back to that teenager, ten-year-old or worst still that five-year-old gripped by the hands of fear. When you find yourself regressing to when you first experienced a similar time, with all the physical and mental emotions of that traumatised child, try and handle yourself with compassion.

When a child is fearful, they yearn for the comfort, protection of the parent guardian to protect them from what they believe to be scary and unmanageable. The same is true for adults, if we feel that comfort, security is not available, we too as adults will do what we did as a child. The same can be said for adults, in the absence of comfort and security there can be a tendency to default to the behaviour of a child.

We may cry, cower, bury our head in the sand or simply switch off. Adults who regress tend to beat up on themselves or feel embarrassed. They make excuses for their behaviour and ultimately miss the point. What you did not handle as a child, you will handle and complete as an adult; should you skip learning to tie your laces as a child, rest assured you will master it as an adult.

Your 'Attitude' Will Determine Your 'Altitude'

If your attitude is good, you will obtain good results, if it is excellent then you will obtain excellent results. However, if it is bad you will obtain bad results. If it is neither good nor bad the same applies, the trick is to be true to self. Take time out to examine where you are today and make a conscious decision as to where you would like to be.

> "At any given moment you have the power to say: this is not how the story is going to end."
> — Christine Mason Miller

Once done, prioritise that area of your life that needs to be addressed and begin to make degrees of change. Imagine a rocket leaving earth heading for the moon. If it was 3 degrees off at launch it would never reach the moon, however by making degrees of change it could get back on track, the same applies to you.

Use today to commence your healing process and reclaim the adult in you. So, the next time you feel yourself regressing to child mode, start counting from 5 down and make the adult choice. You will be amazed to find out how well this little life hack works.

Reflection:

_____

Action

1.

2.

3.

Positive Affirmation to Self

7. Know Who You Are, Know Yourself

If you give something your best shot and it does not produce the desired outcome that you expected, *what do you do? What does it mean? Does it mean that it was not meant to be? What if you are still determined to make it happen?* The short answer is to know yourself, know who you are! It is only when you know who you are that you will find the faith you need to get where you want to be and do what you need to do.

When you know who you are, it eliminates the guesswork in life; it takes away the need for short cuts, hoping, wishing and trying. When you know who you are you become focused, you know that there is always room for self-improvement and that opens the door for opportunity, new insights and new information.

When you know who you are, you know that what you learn at any given moment will assist you and guide you on the path to where you want to be. <u>When you know yourself</u>, you know your strengths, you embrace your weaknesses and you know that everything is pointing you in the right direction. The direction of learning more, embracing more information about exactly who you are. <u>When you know who you are</u>, you are always grateful, you adopt an attitude of gratitude, you are grateful for all that you have seen, all that you have done, all that you have lost and all that you have received. <u>When you know who you are</u>, you know that in this very perfect moment, all that you are is more than enough to answer any questions you might have about where to go and what to do. <u>When you know who you are</u>, you understand your **S.H.A.P.E.**

S...Spiritual Gifts: not given for your own benefit but for the benefit of others.

H...Heart: your heart reveals the real you, who you truly are, not who others think you are or what circumstances force you to be.

A...Abilities: each and every one of us has been blessed with dozens of untapped abilities, the secret is to unleash and utilise them.

P…Personality: know yours and understand that you are unique with a specific plan that only you can fulfil.

E…Experience: employing your experiences to help yourself and others.

Aldous Huxley said, "*Experience is not what happens to you. It is what you do with what happens to you*". *What will you do with what you have been through?* Do not waste your pain, use it to help others.

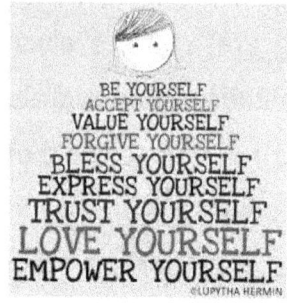

Reflection:

_____
_____
_____
_____
_____
_____
_____
_____
_____
_____
_____

Action

1.

2.

3.

Positive Affirmation to Self

8. You Have Got To WORK At It!!!

Recently I read an article which went something like this

Job Scam Alert

*It is a programme where you work your butt off for someone else for 40 hours a week and sometimes even more. For those 40 years, you get a £60.00 gold watch - if you are lucky - and then try to live on 40% of what you could not live on while you were working 40 hours a week, also known as "a job". This J.O.B is known to leave people **Just Over Broke** after participating for 40 or more years, yet millions yet millions of people fall for it every day.*

> **On Earning:** "Never depend on single income. Make investment to create a second source".
>
> **On Spending:** "If you buy things you do not need, soon you will have to sell things you need".
>
> **On Savings:** "Do not save what is left after spending, but spend what is left after saving".
>
> **On Taking Risk:** "Never test the depth of river with both the feet".
>
> **On Investment:** "Do not put all eggs in one basket".
>
> **On Expectations:** "Honesty is very expensive gift. Do not expect it from cheap people".

Very interesting, I thought, however if millions of people fall for it what can be done to remedy the situation. It has been said that Proper Planning Prevents Poor Performance and managing your **FINANCES** can lead to a healthy retirement as we have all been told. Start early, sit back and maintain.

If you fail to plan you plan to fail.

- Do you have a financial plan?
- Is it written down?
- When was it last reviewed?
- Will it do what you want it to do?
- Words of wisdom from Warren Buffet....

In all what we do, we trade our time for money with an expectation that all will be well, along the journey many will become disillusioned and resentful of the very means that allows them to live the lifestyle they have created for themselves.

Retirement: It's nice to get out of the rat race, but you have to learn to get along with less cheese.

It has been said, most people work hard enough not to get fired and paid just enough money not to quit. Be the change you want to see, under promise and over deliver in all areas of your life. From today make the rest of your life the best of your life and experience life on your own terms.

Reflection:

_____
_____
_____
_____
_____
_____
_____
_____
_____
_____
_____

Action

1.

2.

3.

Tony Henry

Positive Affirmation to Self

9. Perception vs Reality

Have you ever noticed how some people have a way of acting as if their life is not their own responsibility? At the drop of a hat they can give you chapter and verse, point by point why they have been unable to do whatever because of whom ever. You will notice that in these situations there will be no accountability for the part they played in creating the situation(s) they find themselves in.

> *People see what they want to see and what people want to see never has anything to do with the truth.*
> --ROBERTO BOLAÑO

Their story may sound reasonable, you may even try to empathise with them, yet somewhere in the back of your mind you know what you know. The only reason this person does not have the life they want is because somewhere in the back of *their* mind, there is a belief system that says they do not believe they deserve it. This could be around things as simple as their lifestyle, money, relationship, career or leisure. Faced with this reality a decision needs to be made. If doing what you have always done, fails to get you what you want, it is time for change, it is time to ask for help. It is time to find an agency, of some sort, that will support you in making the right decisions. It will mean watching and reading the programmes or material that will help you to grow. You see, life works in cycles and believe it or not, for those of us who are prepared to acknowledge our shortcomings, there is a grace period for change. When we are ready to be accountable for our deeds and actions. When we are ready to forgive and receive forgiveness. When we are ready to make amends with that veil of darkness, that feeling of *"woe is me"* will be lifted. The blinkers will be removed and the ability to see what we have been wanting to see, and experience what we have wanted to experience, will be presented. The only thing that will be left will be for us to step into our greatness and disallow our past from holding us back. Kicking into touch the negative statements our parents might have said about each other or money and conquering those skeletons in the closet.

> Change the story and you change perception; change perception and you change the world.
> — Jean Houston

When that day, that season arrives resist the temptation to remain in conflict with your perceived life story, look at your reality, and look at your truth. Then you will see how real it is.

Reflection:

Action

1.

2.

3.

Positive Affirmation to Self

10. Time Out To Love Self

When was the last time you took some serious time out for yourself, reconnecting and reflecting where you have come from and where you see your future?

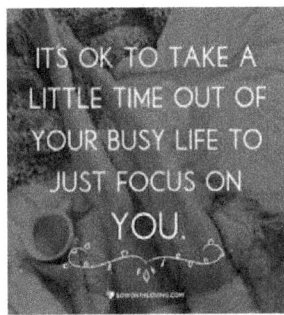

Start by taking some time out, maybe just 10 or 15 minutes reflecting on a breakthrough that you have experienced. This could be passing your driving test or exam, being successful at work with a project, overcoming a barrier to attain a goal like skydiving or even climbing a mountain. Then, reconstructing your journey taking the positive lessons of how you made it through. Celebrate whatever successes you have achieved then love, hug and reward self. Today make some time to practice rewarding yourself for making it through to another day. Hey! Treat yourself to your favourite coffee and a muffin if that is your thing. Challenge!!!

What I am about to ask you may sound a little off the chart but it could save your life, if you take it seriously enough.

Doing this one thing will make such a difference in you that you may not recognise yourself thereafter.

Here it is...

For the next forty days, write a daily love letter and send it to yourself and before you shake your head and refuse to do it, allow the idea to wash over you. When was the last time you had hot, passionate, steamy love coming at you on a daily basis? We all profess to wanting love or to be in love, however, how much love can you stand? *For God so loved the world that He gave up His only begotten Son, so that whoever believes in Him should not perish but have everlasting life* - John 3:16.

> Eat like you love yourself.
>
> Move like you love yourself.
>
> Speak like you love yourself.
>
> Act like you love yourself.

So, if God so loved the world that he gave his only son, what is it that will prevent you from demonstrating love to and for yourself. Just for today, and for the next forty days, be the object of your own love. Send yourself a love letter and then take the time to read it to yourself. Once you get it down to a science, you may feel loving enough to share some of the same loving thoughts with someone else. (Adapted from *Until Today! - Daily Devotions for Spiritual Growth and Peace of Mind*, Iyanla Vanzant, ISBN 0-671-03766-8)

Reflection:

_____
_____
_____
_____
_____
_____
_____
_____
_____
_____
_____

Action

1.

2.

3.

Positive Affirmation to Self

11. Don't Stay Stuck

Don't stay stuck, easier said than done. In an age and time where many, due to life's challenges, feel stuck and knowing how to move forward appears to be mystifying. It is as if you are being held back. Someone or something is holding you back, preventing you from pursuing your dreams. You feel limited and do not know what to do.

You feel you have no idea how to break free from the situation you find yourself in. It is quite scary to be confronted by an invisible foe you cannot seem to tackle or get to grips with. Even though your current situation may appear hopeless to you, there is much you can do about it. Do not stay stuck where you are, keep growing. The trick is to make a decision to develop better habits, to have better relationships and create a better life. Always remember, you are the captain of your ship and it is your responsibility to chart your course through all that life throws at you.

> It's never too late to start over. If you weren't happy with yesterday, try something different today. Don't stay stuck, do better.

Here are a few suggestions to get you started:

Differentiate between feelings and facts

You feel as if you are stuck in life. Therefore, you conclude you cannot move on. Sometimes however, your emotions might not be telling the (entire) truth. The inability to get unstuck may feel very real but in the end, it is just a feeling. Feelings are created from the stories you tell yourself in your mind and these very feelings create your perception of the situation. For this reason, it is important to remind yourself that feelings are not facts. They are just an aspect of what you are thinking. Try to look at your situation more objectively. Emotional responses, are a reaction to your feelings which can cloud your perception of reality. Feeling stuck in life could be a response to exaggerated expectations or mere fantasies.

Stop Making Excuses

Excuses keep us from moving forward in life. Do not allow excuses to keep you right where you are. Stop trying to rationalise why you cannot get on with your life. Do not focus on all the different reasons that keep you stuck. Shift your attention to what needs to be done to effect positive change. Believe you can do it, visualise doing it and then do it. Your attention goes where energy flows. Liberate your mind then your life will follow.

Be Grateful for What You Have

You may feel as if you are not moving forward when you think you are yet to accomplish certain things in life. As a result, you get frustrated about your situation and feel as if your stuck. Being grateful for what you already have can help you to ease the feeling of being stuck. By the thought of gratitude alone, your body produces two powerful chemicals, dopamine and oxytocin. These can help you rediscover what is beautiful about your life. Instead of focusing on what you do not have, start focusing and being grateful for all you do have. Count your blessings and be open to receive even more.

Let go!

The things that keep you stuck most often lie in the past. If you want to get your act together, letting go of your thoughts, feelings and emotions of the past is a great place to start. It does not matter that your parents were not loving or that your husband / wife cheated on you. Stand back, let go of the sadness surrounding it and observe the thoughts of your past for what they were, an episode of your life which you survived. Make time to celebrate your progress, understand that you are an overcomer and your best is yet to come.

Reflection:

_____
_____
_____
_____
_____
_____
_____
_____
_____
_____
_____
_____

Action

1.

2.

3.

Positive Affirmation to Self

12. Change: Mind, Body And Spirit

In order to create lasting change mentally, physically and spiritually we must be in alignment or being consistent with our thoughts and actions. If or when we are not, one or more aspects of our inner being will work against us. When this happens, it becomes very difficult to achieve that which we say we desire.

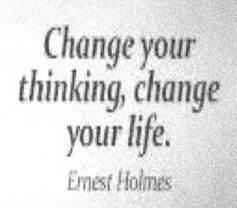
Change your thinking, change your life.
Ernest Holmes

It is not enough to think about the good things we want such as, cars, houses and holidays, we must also feel good about what we want. It is not enough to just want to forget about unpleasant experiences such as divorce, redundancy and major illness we must also work to change how we feel about them.

In order to eliminate negative thoughts and feelings, we must shift what we think. When we shift how we think, we change how we feel and what we believe. When we change our stinking

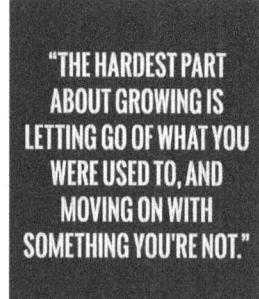
"THE HARDEST PART ABOUT GROWING IS LETTING GO OF WHAT YOU WERE USED TO, AND MOVING ON WITH SOMETHING YOU'RE NOT."

thinking and let go of all our negative thoughts, feelings and experiences, we open ourselves up for forgiveness, healing and a new learning which in turn allows for positive change to take place.

With positive change we open ourselves to be filled with positive thoughts, feelings and new experiences of what it is we say we truly desire **Love, Peace, Joy** and **Happiness.**

The Monday Morning Fix

Reflection:

_____
_____
_____
_____
_____
_____
_____
_____
_____
_____

Action

1.

2.

3.

Positive Affirmation to Self

13. Control Or Controlled

In a dog-eat-dog environment, where people are being hurt or are in fear of being hurt, they try to gain control of the situation they find themselves in by manipulating situations for personal gain. They may even try to gain control of you! If a person distrusts their ability to stay in control, they will attempt to govern everything and everyone around.

When a person feels wronged or is afraid of being wrong, they will endeavour to do everything and anything to ensure  everything goes the way they want it to go. They realise that the only way to have that kind of power is to be in control. Control comes in many guises it can be in your face or sweet and seductive. It is imperative that whatever guise it comes in, you are able to see it for what it is and recognise when you in turn fall foul.

Know the Signs:

- You are fighting to prove your right.

- You lie to prove your right.
- You have a need to be right.
- You are yelling in order to be heard.
- The only view that makes sense is yours.
- The only thing that matters is what matters to you.
- You are still giving reasons why? After someone has said no.
- You think if someone gets what they want or need you will not get what you want or need.
- You jump on someone else's case to keep them off yours.
- You believe someone can and will hurt you and you are trying to avoid it.

To date, you might have been unaware how the fear of being hurt or wrong has influenced your decisions, thoughts and your daily walk. As from right now, check yourself for the symptoms of control listed above, be devoted to becoming aware of the things you do to obtain and maintain control!! If you are struggling to get there by yourself, enlist the services of a coach - often termed Life Coach with the focus of helping you discover your truth around your challenges and life goals.

Reflection:

_____
_____
_____
_____
_____
_____
_____
_____
_____
_____

_____

Action

1.

2.

3.

Positive Affirmation to Self

14. Money! Money! Money!

Money can't buy happiness. But somehow, it's much more comfortable to cry in a Lamborghini than on a bicycle.

Is it a rich man's world? Love it, loathe it, save it or blow it, the choice is yours but you simply cannot ignore it. When it speaks, people listen...often without interrupting. It can help you realise or derail your dreams. Importantly, it most definitely counts. When it comes to money, its fundamentals remain constant.

The basics are simple, truth hasn't changed, our environment and how we function continually changes but the basics do not. Spring always follows Winter, water always runs downhill, and the sun will always rise in the East. These are essential truths and it has been this way throughout recorded history. So too are the fundamentals that govern money. Paying yourself first, saving for a rainy day and never spending more than you earn - is wisdom for any age.

Money is a reward you receive for the service you render and the more value you offer, the greater your reward.

Thinking of ways, you can be of greater service to your customers, employers and employees will not only help you earn more money, it will enable you to grow intellectually and ethically if your focus is on the greater good. A focus on value creation is the hallmark of success. Retirement, university expenses, buying a home, a better quality of life, getting in shape, paying off debt, or starting and growing a business, whatever it is, start by knowing your goals and the relationship you have with money.

Adding value to your customers' needs and creating an environment conducive to your employees is an awesome position to start from and maintain growth. A good example of one such company would be Google. Undeniably, one of the most ethical companies in the world. Google, offers countless benefits to its employees of all ranks, but the biggest of them all is probably the relaxed, creativity-oriented approach they apply at their workplaces which looks like more fun than getting-things-done oriented.

Reflection:

_____
_____
_____
_____
_____
_____
_____
_____
_____
_____
_____
_____

Action

1.

2.

3.

Positive Affirmation to Self

15. The Essence Of Self

Once you put yourself on the path to knowing and embracing self and honouring who you are without excuses, defences or limitations, you will experience the power of self-enlightenment, realising who you truly are. And as we take the time to examine why it is and what it is we were born to do, the how unravels and reveals a path of total illumination full of purpose and passion.

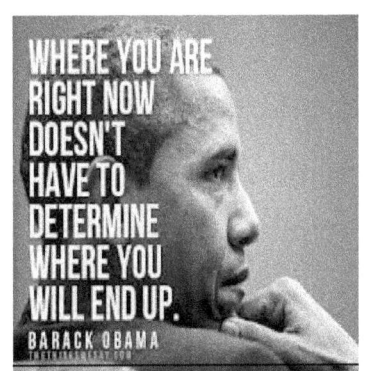

Sounds too out there - too hard, too simple. On the path of knowing oneself, we sometimes struggle to fully understand what is happening with and to us. We even question our worthiness for all the good things that happen to us? As for the bad, that will make us even dislike who we are even more. Maybe you have begun to believe the lies you have been told like you are not smart enough, tall enough, strong enough, academically-sound enough, come from the wrong side of town, wrong school, college or university. Whatever it is that has been spoken against you, remember you have a choice to accept or reject which does not support, compliment or develop your well-being and growth.

Each and every one of us are born into enlightenment, we know everything we need to know and are equipped to do everything we need to do. What many of us lack is the *can-do* mentality. Why? Because we choose to compare with the incomparable, we choose to default to lack rather than gain. *"I can do this."* Opens the door. *"I can't do this."* Closes the door.

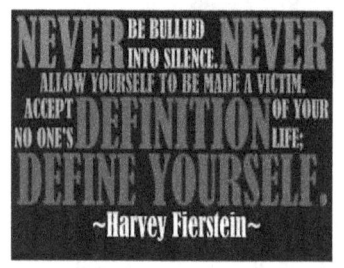

By changing just one letter, we dimmed our internal light and the destruction begins. The light of your enlightenment is already within you, it is the same light that will help you realise the power of your being. It is powered by your thoughts and your words, and what you believe will have a direct effect on how you feel. Each time you are able to acknowledge, accept and embrace the truth about yourself, your internal light becomes brighter. Truth is, it never goes out, the light you see in others is a reflection of the light within yourself. When you realise your own power and stop borrowing the light from others, you will have reached **The Essence of Self.**

Reflection:

_____
_____
_____
_____
_____
_____
_____
_____
_____
_____
_____

_____

Action

1.

2.

3.

Positive Affirmation to Self

16. Withholding Your Feelings

When in a relationship withholding your feelings can and often will lead to detrimental consequences 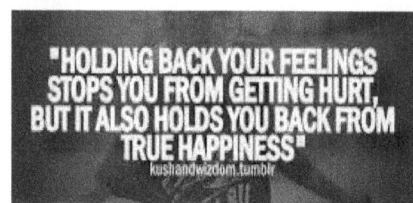 like a breakdown in communication. An unexpressed feeling can be likened to a rubber band that is being stretched to its limit. The longer the feeling is held, the more the tension grows. Eventually something has to give or the band snaps. When this happens, someone gets hurt. Some of the common reasons why some people hold onto their hurt feelings and emotions may be to avoid conflict. You sense that the feeling is wrong since the last time you shared what you felt, it was rejected. That rejection left a bitter taste or memory with you. You decide you are not going to run the risk of upsetting someone to experience their anger, so you internalise your feelings at your own expense.

Yet, trying to avoid conflict does not prevent the hurt, harbouring grudges or resentment. One of the sad realities is that anger is a common response to feeling hurt and if not discharged, tends to increase, distancing the hurt person from the perceived offender.

When trying to protect your mate or other people from your feelings, you probably believe they are unable to handle it or that you do not want to hurt or upset them. Unfortunately, your plan does not work since they are already upset!! The reason - they already know there is something you need to say and in not saying it only creates further tension.

Michael Kolevzon, Professor of Social Work, Virginia Commonwealth University, states: *"Marriage has become the forum for the negotiation of a balance between two conflicting needs: the desire for intimacy on one hand and the need to establish one's identity as a separate person on the other."*

> Always express your true feelings to the ones who really matter to you, because opportunities are lost in the blink of an eye but our regrets can last a lifetime.
> *healthythoughts.in*

Negotiations cannot occur without the wounded party stating his/her hurt as hard as it may seem. Many partners actually find that voicing an old or recent hurt is a relief that frees them to communicate and regain intimacy.

Moving forward we all need to understand that harbouring thoughts and feelings, especially negative ones, are not conducive to our wellbeing. You may not have realised that what you feel is important and that expressing it is an important step to healing yourself and someone else.

Honour yourself by taking the decision to seek help and support in releasing and expressing those thoughts, feelings and emotions that have kept you in bondage. Take time out where possible to be still with yourself and seek guidance in finding the appropriate words and the right opportunity to share your feelings with others and to be healed.

You may want to consider taking a walk whenever there is conflict, so that you are able to emotionally withdraw and take stock of how you are feeling. It will also give you time to be more relaxed and in a better place to respond.

Reflection:

_____
_____
_____
_____
_____
_____
_____
_____
_____
_____
_____
_____

Action

1.

2.

3.

The Monday Morning Fix

Positive Affirmation to Self

17. What Type Are You?

N.I.P.A = Non-Income Producing Activities

I.P.A = Income Producing Activities

N.I.P.A has many traits of paralysis analysis in that if you are not careful you will find yourself doing a lot of preparation without taking any action. e.g. From a business perspective, you know there are calls to make so you decide to create a spreadsheet, so far so good, formatting it in a certain way, still not too bad. However, you then decide it needs to be colour coded, highlighted and the columns equally spaced. Are you beginning to understand?

Income Producing Activities

Treat them like an extremely overweight man treats his trip to the pastry shop.

Nothing gets in the way!

So, having spent a couple of hours on the spreadsheet you now decide that your desk is a mess and the office is in need of organising, so you begin to tidy both. Biggest drawback, not one call has been made. When we, then look at I.P.A (Income Producing Activity), the count is a big fat zero and thus N.I.P.A (Non-Income Producing Activity) wins hands down.

Now on the flip side, is making the calls to clients and closing the business, include asking for referrals in order to get recommendations for more business and to broaden your customer base.

I.P.A: Delivering effective staff training, allowing them to excel in their chosen fields, boosting confidence, motivation and wellbeing - leading to increased productivity. Unsubscribing from email lists that no longer have any benefit or serve a purpose, frees up your time to be more productive. Utilising a power hour where you take no calls and focus on the task at hand and remembering to reward yourself on successful completion.

> OVERTHINKING A SITUATION OR A DECISION CAN LEAD TO A PHENOMENON CALLED ANALYSIS PARALYSIS WHICH RESULTS IN NO DECISION BEING MADE.

Income Producing Activities

Treat them like an extremely overweight person treats their trip to the bakery. **Nothing gets in the way!**

Reflection:

_____
_____
_____
_____
_____
_____
_____
_____
_____
_____
_____

Action

1.

2.

3.

Positive Affirmation to Self

18. Failure To Thrive (FTT)

Having recently completed a Mental Health First Aid Course, I came across a new phrase whilst doing some research on the subject. It is 'FTT', which stands for 'Failure To Thrive'. Psychologists have begun to debate it as perhaps today's largest mental health problem, and it is rapidly growing. Due to discontentment with work life balance.

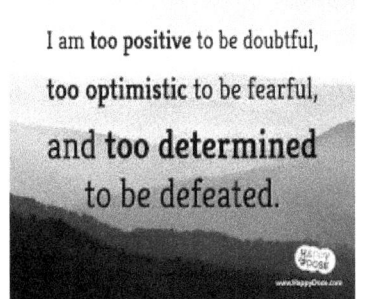

When you have it, you are still able to function but lose your sense of hope and meaning (drive, determination and desire to fulfil your purpose). FTT is not the presence of mental illness; it is the absence of mental, spiritual and emotional vitality. Put another way it is weariness of the soul and the inability to be happy in life. It is that feeling of knowing there is much more to life but you take little or no action and for example, you remain in a dead-end job or relationship.

Want to hear some good news? There is "HOPE." We are all placed on this planet to thrive and to flourish so that people can be encouraged, gardens can be planted, music and books can be written, sick people can be healed, young people can be educated, communities rebuilt, jobs created, loved ones celebrated and life experienced from a balanced perspective.

Starting from today set your intention to be grateful for what you have, be open to receive what is possible. Only you have the power to create the changes that you want to make.

Reflection:

_____
_____
_____
_____
_____
_____
_____
_____
_____
_____

_____

Action

1.

2.

3.

Positive Affirmation to Self

19. Feel The Fear And Do It Anyway

Have you noticed that as soon as you make that decision for change it is as if someone opened the floodgates for analysis paralysis. Imagine you are wanting to open a business of your own and you share the idea with friends and family. You are made redundant with a golden handshake and decide that the time is right for your new venture. All of a sudden everyone has an opinion as to why the timing is not right. Then you start finding ways to convince yourself that you do not have all the skills required to launch your business - the economy is not right, too much competition, you do not have any customers and what the hell was you thinking. These feelings of uneasiness and unsteadiness cause you to squander precious time and to lose the opportunity.

What is the root cause of this all too prevalent mental malaise? **F.E.A.R** - **False Evidence Appearing Real**. So, what is the solution? **F.A.I.T.H** or **Full Acceptance in Trust** and **HOPE**.

When we are in a state of **FEAR** we limit what we can receive because we are closed but when we transition to a state of **FAITH,** we open ourselves to receive all that we desire.

A wise man once said, *"If we do not learn from the past, we are doomed to repeat it."* It is okay to look back and learn but if you drive a car looking in the rearview mirror, you will end up in a ditch. Another way of saying this: *"If we do what we have always done, we will get what we always got."* Whether good or bad, do not get stuck in the past.

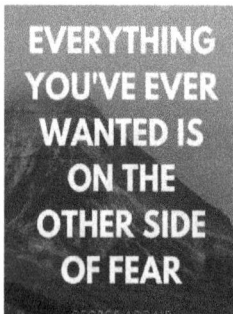

Going forward focus on three things:

1. Decide what is important. Make a decision and stick with it.

2. Prioritise your time. Base your life decisions on your priorities and if you need help figuring out what they are, ask a coach, a mentor or trusted friend.

3. Learn to motivate yourself. To succeed in life, you must learn to encourage, pray and build yourself up.

Once you make the decision to change and transform your life for the better, not everybody will be happy about your success. People's opinions are often fickle, so here is a response you need to adopt.

If it is to be, it is up to me. Success, money and happiness comes easily to me.

The Monday Morning Fix

Reflection:

_____
_____
_____
_____
_____
_____
_____
_____
_____
_____

Action

1.

2.

3.

Positive Affirmation to Self

20. Attitude

"It is your attitude, not your aptitude that determines your altitude."
Zig Ziglar

Said another way: *Your success in life (altitude) is determined more by your desire to succeed (attitude) than by your natural talents (aptitude).*

The longer I live, the more I realise the impact of attitude on life. Attitude, to me, is more important than facts. It is more important than the past, than education, than money, than circumstances, than failure, than successes, than what other people think, say or do.

I believe attitude is more important than appearance, giftedness or skill. It will make or break a company, church or home. Failing to commit and having a negative attitude is like a bad apple, it will spoil the whole bunch. The remarkable thing is, we can choose as to what kind of attitude we embrace each and every day. We cannot change the inevitable. The only thing we can do is play on the one strength we have, and that is our attitude. I am convinced that life is 10% of what happens to you and 90% of how you react to it. Since you alone have control over your attitude, exercising control and adjusting your attitude from the inside, allows your outwardly behaviour to follow.

It is my opinion that we all enter life with the tools we require to fulfil our true potential. If we are prepared to mirror the success of those who have gone before us, not wavering, staying focused with a determination that says: *"I can therefore I will"* and accepting that quitting is not an option the outcome is **SUCCESS**.

> "A Great Attitude becomes a great day which becomes a great month which becomes a great year which becomes a Great LIFE."
> — mandy hale

The Monday Morning Fix

Reflection:

_____
_____
_____
_____
_____
_____
_____
_____
_____
_____
_____

Action

1.
2.
3.

Tony Henry

Positive Affirmation to Self

21. Change Your Password, Change Your Life

In life, we are frequently faced with decisions that impact on our lives, both positively and negatively. The trick is to develop the confidence to seize the opportunities when they are presented since the difference between ordinary and extraordinary, are based on the decisions we make and the eventual opportunities we take. Let me share John's story…

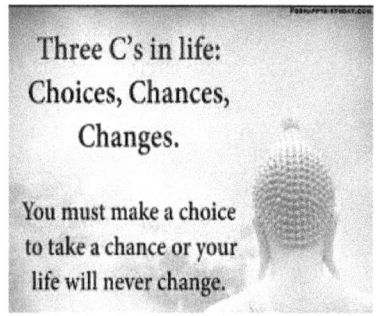

I was stuck in the middle of a pretty bad depression due to my divorce. One day, I walked into the office and my computer screen showed the following message:

> Your password has expired. Click **Change password** to change your password.

I read this dumb message in my mind with an angry grandpa voice:

> "…The password has expired again."

Every 30 days the Microsoft Exchange Server is configured to ask employees to change their passwords. Annoyingly, the server forces us to use at least one uppercase character, at least one lowercase character, at least one symbol and at least one number.

Oh, and the whole thing cannot be less than 8 characters and you cannot use any of the same passwords that have been used in the last 3 months. I was furious since I was late for work and had a very important meeting to attend. In my mind, I was telling myself that having to change my password was going to be a huge waste of time.

However, as the input field prompted me to type my password, a little voice said, *"Change your password, change your life."* It was obvious that I could not focus on getting things done with my current lifestyle where I played the victim or failed to take responsibility for my actions. Of course, there were clear indicators of what I needed to do, to regain control of my life but when your head is filled with negative thoughts, it is easy to miss the clues.

My password became: *Forgive@h3r.* I would have to type this statement in several times a day. Each time I typed in my new password I would quietly say forgive her and the more I forgave, the better I felt. In the following weeks my mood dramatically improved. One month later, the exchange server asked me again to renew my password. I thought about the next thing I would like to get done.

My password became: *Quit@smoking4ever,* and guess what happened? I quit smoking overnight. This password was a challenge, so to the side effects of not smoking was not easy 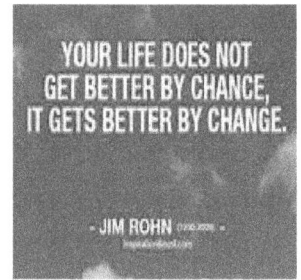 to cope with but I did it by focusing on the health benefits. The amount of money I saved, motivated me to see it through. One month later, my password became: *Save4trip@thailand* and guess where I went? Thailand, 3 months later - with savings. I kept doing this repeatedly month after month, with great results. So, I learnt that I can truly change my life if I play it right. Here are some of my passwords from the last two years, so you get an idea of how my life has changed, thanks to this method:

Forgive@her (to my ex-wife, who started it all)

Quit@smoking4ever (It worked)

Save4trip@thailand (It worked)

Eat2times@day (It never worked; I am still fat)

Sleep@before12 (It worked)

Ask@her4date (It worked and I fell in love again)

No@drinking2months (It worked. I feel better)

Get@c4t! (It worked and now I have a beautiful cat)

Facetime2mom@Sunday (It worked and I talk with my mum every week)

And the one for last month:

Save4@ring (Yep. Life is going to change again, soon)

> "THE HARDEST PART ABOUT GROWING IS LETTING GO OF WHAT YOU WERE USED TO, AND MOVING ON WITH SOMETHING YOU'RE NOT."

I still anxiously await each month to change my password into something I need to get done. This method has consistently worked for me and I have shared it with a few close friends and relatives. I did not think it was a breakthrough in tiny-habits but it did have a great impact on my life. If you try it with the right mindset and attitude, maybe it could help change your life, too.

Reflection:

_____
_____
_____
_____
_____
_____
_____
_____
_____
_____

_____

Action

1.

2.

3.

Positive Affirmation to Self

22. We Are Like Pencils

Five things you need to know before you go out into the world. One day the pencil maker was talking to his pencils before putting them into the box.

He said to them, "There are five things you need to know before I send you out into the world. Always remember them and you will become the best pencils you can be."

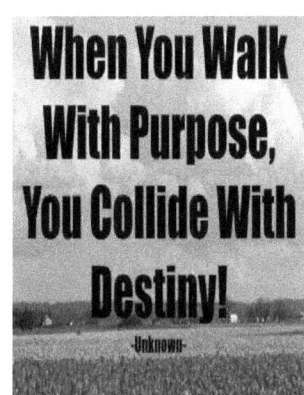

1. You will be able to do many great things but only if you allow yourself to be held in someone's hand.

2. You will experience a painful sharpening from time to time, but you will need it to become a better pencil.

3. You will be able to correct any mistake you make.

4. The most important part of you will always be what is inside.

5. On every surface you are used on, you must leave your mark. No matter what the condition, you must continue to write.

The pencils understood their purpose and promised to remember their maker's words and got into the box. We are like a pencil. The Creator made us for a purpose. The question is, have we understood what that purpose in life is?

"We are what we repeatedly do, excellence then is not an act but a habit"
Aristotle

Tony Henry

Reflection:

_____
_____
_____
_____
_____
_____
_____
_____
_____
_____
_____

Action

1.

2.

3.

Positive Affirmation to Self

23. The Rule Of ONE
Focus and Follow One Course Until Successful

Rather than spread your Goals or Resolutions, follow the rule of **ONE**...

Focusing on the One Goal or Resolution keeps it simple. It minimises any fuss and creates a win-win scenario. When you are able to prioritise, the best use of your time you create a sense of urgency and in doing so, you are able to combine the best use of your gifts, talents and abilities to achieve it. When you apply the **ARC** principle **Accountability, Responsibility** and **Consistency** You cement your intentions and increase your potential for success.

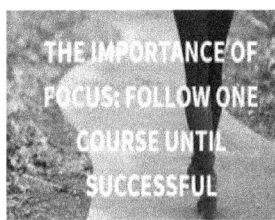

Accountability:

Serves to protect your character as well as your credibility. By focusing on the **ONE** Goal or Resolution, you remove complexity, replacing it with confidence and control. Making yourself accountable to someone you know, respect and trust, keeps you in check and when you set the rules of engagement your accountability is secured.

Responsibility:

Implementation is key, it is worth saying loud and proud that *"Goals / Resolutions never fail, it is all about the implementation."* Having decided on the **ONE** Goal or Resolution, it is your responsibility to ensure that you do everything humanly possible to stay on track until you succeed.

> You get what you focus on, so focus on what you want.

Consistency:

Is where the magic happens. By mapping out your Daily Method of Operation (**DMO**) you set the success wheels in motion. Just like muscle memory repetition is the mother of all learning. As you create this new culture of success you will be able to replicate your results to suit each challenge you set yourself. The end result is you begin realising your dreams and fulfilling your potential. No matter your goal, whether it be getting out of debt, a new job, starting a new business, relationship or getting into the best shape of your life, there is no singular goal you cannot accomplish with this strategy. And that is the magic of focusing on the **ONE**.

Goals or Resolutions never fail, it is the lack of execution.

The Monday Morning Fix

Reflection:

Action

1.

2.

3.

Tony Henry

Positive Affirmation to Self

24. Work To Live Or Live To Work

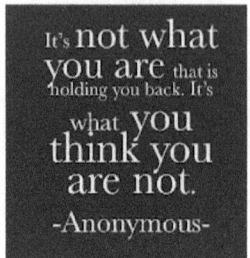

It's not what you are that is holding you back. It's what you think you are not.
-Anonymous-

Work to live or live to work, that is the question? Most of us do not work because we want to, we work because we think we have to. We all do it, in varying degrees and sometimes forget that the work we do does not define us. Our work is not who we are, it is what we do. Life is all about balance and in order to find that balance we have to understand the rules of the game.

So, what does balance look like? It includes having fun, enjoying yourself, laughing, joking and not taking everything personally. Taking time out, resting, pressing that pause button, catching forty winks, stilling the mind, getting a good night's sleep. How about a bit of mindfulness and meditation, getting still and being aware of where you are and what is going on within the confines of you?

What forms of physical activity do you engage in? How does it fit with your lifestyle and your life walk? How are you mentally stimulating your mind? Have you become stagnant or are you a fountain of youth devouring all within your path and making the most of every opportunity? When was the last time you were truly stimulated to push beyond your comfort zone to experience the satisfaction of mental and emotional growth? Work is necessary. However, it should not be at the expense of self, family,  relationships, values, health or morality. All work and no play may give us a substantial bank balance but it can be at the cost of all that we say we love and cherish.

Reflection:

_____
_____
_____
_____
_____
_____
_____
_____
_____
_____
_____

Action

1.

2.

3.

Positive Affirmation to Self

25. Time Is The Master

Time can be viewed very differently depending on your viewpoint. To demonstrate this point, allow me to share this story with you:

Time has a wonderful way of showing us what really matters.

One person worked long and hard making a great career. One day he decided to rest and live in luxury for his pleasure, which he could afford because of the wealth he accumulated. Just as he made this decision, the Angel of Death came to him. Being a very wealthy person, he thought he could haggle for some more time. So, off he went as best as he could but the angel was unmoved.

Desperate, the rich man made a last proposal: *"Give me just one hour of my life, so that I can admire the beauty of this earth for the last time and spend some time with my family and friends whom I have not seen for a long time, and I'll give you all of my wealth."*

But the angel refused again. Finally, the man asked if the angel could give him at least one minute so that he could write a goodbye note. His wish was granted and this is what he wrote:

"Spend your time, which was given to you, in the right way. I could not buy even an hour of life with all of my wealth. Listen to your heart and check if the things surrounding you have true value. Cherish every minute of your life."

Time is free, but it's priceless. You can't own it, but you can use it. You can't keep it, but you can spend it. Once you've lost it you can never get it back.

We all have 24 hours in any one day, what are you doing with yours?

The Monday Morning Fix

Reflection:

_____
_____
_____
_____
_____
_____
_____
_____
_____
_____

_____

Action

1.

2.

3.

Positive Affirmation to Self

26. Black Or White

Balance can be viewed differently depending on your viewpoint. To demonstrate this allow me to share this life lesson with you:

A young boy's perspective

When I was in elementary school I got into an argument with a girl in my class. I have forgotten what the argument was about but I have never forgotten the lesson I learnt 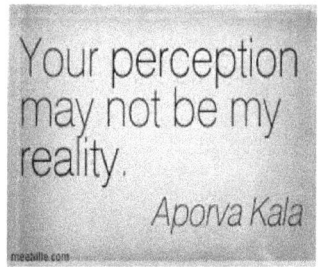 that day. I was convinced that *"I"* was right and *"she"* was wrong and *"she"* was just as convinced that *"I"* was wrong and *"she"* was right. The teacher decided to teach us both a very important lesson. She put us in the front of the class and placed her on one side of her desk and me on the other. In the middle of her desk was a large, round object. She asked me what colour it was. I could clearly see that it was black. She asked the girl what colour the object was. *"White,"* she replied.

I could not believe she said the object was white when it was obviously black! Another argument started between my classmate and I, this time about the *colour* of the object. The teacher told me to go stand where the girl was and told the girl to come stand where I had stood. We changed places. Now she asked me what was the colour of the object. I had to answer *"White."*

> **BALANCE**
> Truly successful decision making relies on a balance between deliberate and instinctive thinking.
> —Malcolm Gladwell

It was an object with two differently colored sides and from my classmate's viewpoint it was white. Yet, from my side it was black.

The moral of the story, before you pass judgment on anyone, ensure you have all the facts, that you can truly say you see what they see and have lived what they have lived.

Reflection:

_____
_____
_____
_____
_____
_____
_____
_____
_____
_____
_____

Action

1.

2.

3.

Tony Henry

Positive Affirmation to Self

27. Life Is Answering Your Requests

Life will accommodate whatever you choose, exactly the way you choose it. Whether or not you believe it, what you have in your life right now is a reflection of your own requests, some of which you made openly and others you made silently. Imagine having some limiting beliefs around money, whereby you are always cutting back because you believe that there is never enough. Eventually, all that you surround yourself with, will be a reflection of the very same.

Life can be like driving on an open road or navigating mountainous terrain. It is like waking up on a sun-filled beach or shivering in the cold of winter. It can be a blessing or a curse. It can be mysterious full of opportunities  or plagued with illness and hurt. Whatever the outcome, everyone has a role to play. Life is very accommodating and the minute your requests change, your life will follow suit. You may not have realised that life is answering your requests. Take a moment and reflect on the conversations you have been having with yourself, focusing on the language, the tone and the temperament.

You see, you may not have believed you have the power or the right to ask for more than what you have right now. You may not believe that you are deserving of better, that your requests should be answered, that your life should be full of abundance and that life should work for you. Just for today, be willing to spend some time on self, create a list of positive, self-affirming requests that empower you to be the best that you can be. Do not hold back, first create them in your mind and then experience the gamut of emotions, the positive feelings that is associated with your thoughts.

Next write them down, detailing every aspect that is of importance to you. Do not be afraid to redraft until what you have on paper is a true reflection of what you had in your mind. Finally, speak them into existence remembering what it is that you have created. If it does not show up, be conscious of your counter requests.

> SPEAK WHAT YOU SEEK UNTIL YOU SEE WHAT YOU'VE SAID

Be devoted to requesting what you truly desire, enabling you to truly experience life on your own terms.

Reflection:

_____
_____
_____
_____
_____
_____
_____
_____
_____
_____
_____
_____

Action

1.

2.

3.

Positive Affirmation to Self

28. Time

"First Thing Every Morning" – 86400 seconds

"If you had a bank that credited your account each morning with £86,400 - with no balance carried from day-to-day - what would you do?" Interesting thought! Well, you do have such a bank...**Time**.

Every morning it credits you with 86,400 seconds. Every night it rules off as *"lost"* whatever you have failed to use toward good purposes. It carries over no balances and allows no overdrafts. You cannot hoard it, save it, store it, loan it or invest it. You can only use it - **Time.**

Here is a story that drives the point home. Arthur Berry was described by *Time* magazine as *"The slickest second-story man in the East"*, truly one of the most famous jewel thieves of all time. In his years of crime, he committed as many as 150 burglaries and stole jewels valued between $5 and $10 million. He seldom robbed from anyone not listed in the Social Register (people with a high net worth) and often did

his work in a tuxedo. On an occasion or two, when caught in the act of a crime by a victim, he charmed his way out of being reported to the police. But like most people who engaged in a life of crime, he was eventually caught, convicted and served 25 years in prison for his crimes. Following his release, he worked as a counterman in a roadside restaurant on the East Coast for $50 a week.

A newspaper reporter found and interviewed him about his life. After talking about his thrilling life episodes, he concluded the interview saying, *"I'm not good at morals. But early in my life I was intelligent and clever, and I got along well with people. I think I could have made something of my life, but I didn't. So, when you write the story of my life, when you tell people about all the burglaries, don't leave out the biggest one of all...Don't just tell them I robbed Jesse Livermore, the Wall Street baron or the cousin of the King of England. You tell them Arthur Berry robbed Arthur Berry."*

Tony Henry

Here is one terrific truth about time:

> ***Time is measurable***
> ***Everybody has the same amount of time***
> ***Pauper or king***
> ***It's not how much time you have***
> ***It's how well you use it***

Reflection:

_____
_____
_____
_____
_____
_____
_____
_____
_____
_____
_____
_____

Action

1.
2.
3.

Tony Henry

Positive Affirmation to Self

29. The Hidden Gemstone

There once was a farmer who lived on a beautiful farm that his family owned for many decades. Eventually, the farmer died and after being in the family for more than two hundred years, the property was sold to one of the neighbours. As the new owner of the farm was walking in the field, he saw a large, unusual-looking rock just barely sticking out of the ground.

He picked it up and began to examine it. Immediately, he could tell that this was no ordinary rock but some type of gemstone. He took it home, washed it and brought it to a jewellery store in the town where he lived. The jeweller confirmed what the owner already suspected, the old stone that had been in that field for thousands of years was a large, uncut emerald that proved to be worth several millions.

Think about this, that gemstone was in the field all along just waiting for someone to come along and *"discover"* it.

Undoubtedly, the emerald had been seen thousands of times before but it was overlooked since it appeared to be nothing more than an ordinary rock. How often do we overlook treasures because of preconceived expectations and personal biases? 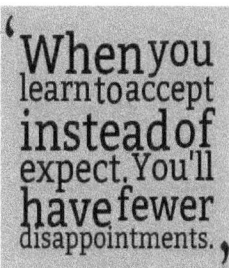 As you seek to find your purpose in life make time to discover your **Skills, Talents and Abilities.** They are the keys that will unlock your potential and release your ability to achieve far beyond what you could ever conceive.

Expectations can come across as pre-meditated resentments.

The Monday Morning Fix

Reflection:

_____
_____
_____
_____
_____
_____
_____
_____
_____
_____

Action

1.

2.

3.

Tony Henry

Positive Affirmation to Self

30 Passion Into Profit

Having recently attended a wealth seminar where the conversation focused on turning your **Passion into Profit.** I found myself asking many questions about my own personal journey, my successes, failures (lessons) and current opportunities. How my own skills, talents and abilities linked into my passion and the million-dollar question - how do I turn them into profit? After spending some time in thought, here are eight tips to start the ball rolling:

1. Get Clear

The first step towards turning **Passion into Profit** is to get clear about what you want. For me, this means drilling down to the thing or things that I enjoy and do best and setting goals that are specific, realistic and have a deadline. What is it that you want from life? Remember the journey of a thousand miles begins with a single step and what the mind can conceive you can achieve.

2. Take Action

You need to be willing to take action. You need to be willing to take steps every single day towards achieving your goals. What's your D.M.O (Daily Method of Operation), decide on what you need to do and program it into your daily routine. Make yourself Accountable, Responsible and Consistent.

3. Model People

One of the best tips I can give you is to model people you know, respect and trust that are currently doing what you would like to do. Think about it, if you decide to mirror what successful people have done to become successful, you will inevitably become successful. Whatever it is, avoid making excuses and take action. There will be no perfect time to go after your dreams, so you might as well start now.

> IF YOU DON'T HAVE BIG DREAMS & GOALS YOU'LL END UP WORKING REALLY HARD FOR SOMEONE WHO DOES.

4. Overcome Your Obstacles

Be aware of your obstacles and limitations. Once you have a very clear goal of what you want to achieve, take a clean sheet of paper and write down the obstacles you think you will face on the path toward your goal. By being true to yourself, you are then able to come up with solutions before the storm clouds begin to circle.

5. Face Your Fears

Going after your passion is not a walk in the park. If it was, more people would live a life of passion and fulfilment. You  can decide to "Face Everything and Rise" or "Forget Everything and Run", the choice is yours. You can choose to buy into your fears and live a life of mediocrity or you can face your fears and experience life on your own terms.

6. Patience

This journey will take a lot of patience. Why? Because challenges will be presented to you. You will have to face your fears, encounter a curve ball or two but you must stay focused (follow one course until successful). Turning your **Passion into Profit** is something that everyone can do but not everyone has the determination or willpower to make it happen. Are you ready and willing to make it happen?

7. Get comfortable in discomfort

Doing something you have never done before can be very scary and uncomfortable. The unknown often becomes an excuse for not moving forward, however allow your fear to empower you not hinder you. Be the change you want to see.

8. Start now, not tomorrow

Life is a journey not a destination, realise that success will not come instantly. All those who have gone before you and made it share a common story of frustration, disappointment, fear, anxiety, hard times, difficulty, hard knocks and misery. However, they never threw in the towel, they persevered to the end and in so doing became the men and women they are today.

> YOU ARE ONLY AS STRONG AS YOU ALLOW YOURSELF TO BE, NEVER GET DISCOURAGED, NEVER GIVE UP. CONSISTENCY & DEDICATION IS THE KEY TO SUCCESS

The Monday Morning Fix

Reflection:

_____
_____
_____
_____
_____
_____
_____
_____
_____
_____

Action

1.

2.

3.

Tony Henry

Positive Affirmation to Self

31. Stay Sharp

At a time where many seem to be struggling to maintain a decent quality of life and work life balance, I am reminded of the story of the woodcutter.

There once was a very strong woodcutter, who asked for a job in a timber merchant company and got it. The pay was really good and so was the working conditions. For those reasons, the woodcutter was determined to do his best. His boss gave him an axe and showed him the area where he was to work. The first day, the woodcutter felled 18 trees.

"Congratulations" the boss said. *"Good job, keep it up."*

Very motivated by the boss's words, the woodcutter tried harder the next day but managing only 15 trees. The third day he tried even harder but could only manage 10 trees. Day after day he was bringing in less and less trees.

"I must be losing my strength", the woodcutter thought.

He went to the boss and apologised, saying he could not understand what was going on.

"When was the last time you sharpened your axe?" The boss asked. *"Sharpen my axe! I have no time to sharpen my axe. I have been very busy trying to cut trees…"*

Reflection

Our lives are like that. We sometimes get so busy we do not take the time to *"sharpen the axe."* In today's world, it seems that everyone is busier than ever, but less happy than ever. Why is that? Could it be that we have forgotten how to stay *"sharp"*?

There is nothing wrong with activity and hard work but we should not get so busy that we neglect the truly important things in life, like making time for family and friends, giving back to the community, realising our dreams and making time for the Creator.

We all need time to relax, to think and meditate, to learn and grow. If we do not take the time to "sharpen the axe", we will become dull and lose our effectiveness.

Nothing beats the satisfaction of a good days pay for a good day's work. The only way to do great work is to love what you do. If you have not found it yet, keep looking. Do not settle. As with all matters of the heart, you will know when you find it.

Reflection:

_____
_____
_____
_____
_____
_____
_____
_____
_____
_____
_____
_____

Action

1.

2.

3.

Positive Affirmation to Self

32 Mistakes Or Lessons In Living

Back in the summer of 2012 I had the fortune / misfortune to do business with someone who I shall not mention, regarding property. It started off extremely well and I could see my life changing for the better. Being able to upgrade my standard of living and acquiring many of the desired items on my vision board. 12 months on and I was minus £200k. Why? I had taken my eye off the prize and got sucked in by the hype. Being chased for money when there is no money is no joke, you either sink or swim and did I learn to swim whether I felt like it or not. That whole experience introduced me to another level of negotiating in order to survive, reinforcing the expression every cloud has a silver lining. A powerful lesson coming from a mistake.

> Your past mistakes are meant to guide you, not define you.

Is it possible to live life without making a mistake? If not, why is it that when you do, the world is more likely to condemn you for it? A mistake is sometimes a lesson in disguise. Therefore, you should not be fearful of making any in your life since you may get to learn a grand lesson.

"Your mistakes are a key part of learning who you are as a person. Thus, a life spent making mistakes is not only more honourable but more useful than a life spent doing nothing."
George Bernard Shaw

Here's a real truth, it is inevitable that you will make mistakes in your life. If you only choose to look at it as a setback, you will miss the opportunity to see the flip side of the lesson. Or that the very same mistake can be seen as a setup for a comeback. All too often, creative solutions come from the mistakes you have made. And when you are able to look at your mistakes as opportunities to better yourself, you open yourself to see and receive solutions to many of the challenges.

Next time you make a mistake, think about what it taught you rather than what it cost you. Remember,

every mistake you make, gives you the opportunity to learn something new.

Reflection:

_____
_____
_____
_____
_____
_____
_____
_____
_____
_____
_____

Action

1.

2.

3.

Tony Henry

Positive Affirmation to Self

33. Seventy Percent

I am reminded of a business tycoon who amassed a fortune and passed away prematurely. His widow, who was left with $1.9bn in the bank, married his chauffeur. His chauffeur said, *"All the while, I thought I was working for my boss... it is only now that I realise, my boss was all the time, working for me!!!"*

The cruel reality is, it is more important to live longer than to have more wealth. So, we must strive to have a strong and healthy body. It really does not matter who is working for whom. In a high-end hand phone, 70% of the functions are 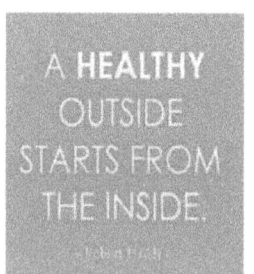 useless! In an expensive car, 70% of the speed and gadgets are not needed! A luxurious villa or mansion, 70% of the space is usually not used or occupied! In your wardrobe of clothes, 70% of them are not worn!

When you measure the time spent at work earning, 70% can be taken up by your immediate family and the upkeep there of. So, if 70% goes out, it is imperative that you make full use of the 30% you get to keep. Go for medical check-ups even if you are not sick. Drink more water, even if you are not thirsty. Learn to let go, even if faced with grave problems. Endeavour to give in, even if you are in the right. Remain humble, even if you are very rich and powerful. Learn to be contented, even when you feel you do not have what you should have. Exercise your mind and body, even if you are very busy. And most importantly make time for the people you care about. Tomorrow is promised to no one.

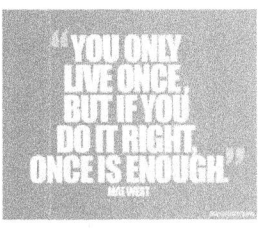

LIVE, LAUGH, LOVE...

Reflection:

_____
_____
_____
_____
_____
_____
_____
_____
_____
_____

_____

Action

1.

2.

3.

Positive Affirmation to Self

34. Miracles Happen

Miracles happen every day for each and every one of us. You have the power to make miracles happen. Take the time to smile at a passer-by or compliment your friend on how they look, something they have achieved or done well.

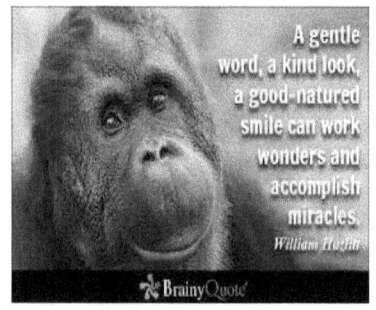

Even though you might not feel at your best, you still have the ability to create a miracle such as a remarkable event or development that brings very welcome consequences. Say, for example, you make the time to call a friend who has been placed on your heart, only to find out that your intervention helped that same friend who was contemplating taking their life. We all experience days that appear to go wrong at every corner, however we hold the key to turning a less than ordinary day into a miraculous one. 'Out of adversity grows miracles.' When we change our perception of what a miracle is, we then have the ability to see them all around us.

When you are in that dark space where nothing seems to be going right, take a moment to close your eyes and picture that last thing that made you happy. Be present in that moment, experience the joy, the happiness and relive it as if you were there right now. Allow that moment to engulf your entire being and give thanks. Depression and joy cannot live in the same house. When you are reliving that positive moment take the opportunity to make that overdue call, do that outstanding task and pat yourself on the back.

It is important to be aware of the world around you. Be open to give and receive love in all its forms, whether that be a hug, a gentle touch or a smile. Understand what your miracles are. Make some time today to appreciate those little miracles and  be prepared to be a miracle for someone in need. You woke up this morning and that is amazing, there were many who failed to be blessed with the gift of another day. Let us not take life for granted, instead let's determine to cherish the little things and hug the ones we love.

The Monday Morning Fix

Not every day will be a great day but great things do happen every day.

Reflection:

_____
_____
_____
_____
_____
_____
_____
_____
_____
_____
_____
_____

Action

1.

2.

3.

Positive Affirmation to Self

35. Failure Is Inevitable

(But does not need to be detrimental)

> YOU CAN BE DISCOURAGED BY FAILURE OR YOU CAN LEARN FROM IT. SO GO AHEAD AND MAKE MISTAKES. MAKE ALL YOU CAN. BECAUSE THAT'S WHERE YOU'LL FIND SUCCESS.

When we remain open, failures can be our stepping stones to success. There are moments in our life where failure is inevitable, but it does not need to be detrimental or dictate the rest of our life. Failures happen just as life happens but they lead us to succeed. Without failure we would never discover a better way of doing that very thing which has eluded us. We often forget that the failures of our past have gotten us to where we are today. Can you recall a failure which has led you onto the road to success? Maybe you lost a job or a client only to gain an even better one. A wise man once said "**When**

> I failed my exam in some subjects and my friend passed. Now he is an engineer in Microsoft and I am the Owner.
> -Bill Gates

one door closes another one opens." It is true and we all have experienced it at least once. Many of the greats in sports and industry have succeeded because they have chosen not to allow failure to define them.

If the likes of Michael Jordan in all his greatness can look at failure in such a positive way, I am sure we all can. Success cannot occur if we do not risk failure, it is with this outlook that we must live our lives, abandon those sentiments that trample your confidence. There is always going to be capability within you, so you have to look within to draw out the skills, honing them until they become great, making you the best you can be.

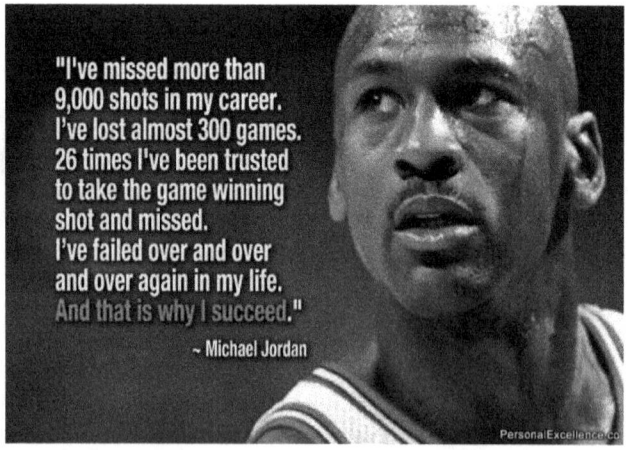

Reflection:

Action

1.

2.

3.

The Monday Morning Fix

Positive Affirmation to Self

36. The Grass Isn't Greener

Have you ever secretly compared your spouse to another man or woman or wished they were more thoughtful, more spiritual, more loving, affectionate, a better kisser or dresser? If you have, let me reassure you the grass is not greener on the other side! We all come with our eccentricities in one form or another, he may leave the toilet seat up but your preference might be to leave it down - truth be known, from a health perspective, it should always be covered to minimise the spread of any bacteria.

Our spouses are the people we fall in love with and often times just need a little encouragement. Instead of comparing and complaining, nurture your mate in the areas they need it most, encourage, edify and build each other up. Raise the bar of expectation to a higher level demonstrating your growth, mentally and spiritually aspire to inspire and reciprocate all that is good.

I heard about a good-looking millionaire who married a plain looking woman, it was the talk of the town. *"Why did he marry her?", "She is not up to his standard" "It won't last!"* When they returned from an extended honeymoon, it looked like the millionaire was with another woman, one glowing with confidence and poise. *"Now that's the kind of wife he deserves"*, declared the town's loud-mouth.

Then she noticed something interesting, it was the same woman. She was completely transformed! Her new husband had taken her away, encouraged and helped to build her self-confidence, till she started to see in her what he had always seen. So instead of walking around on your neighbour's grass, fertilise your own by looking for the good in your spouse.

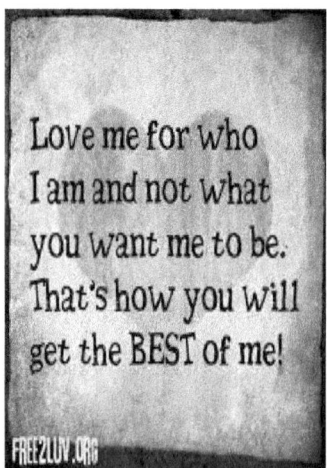

Reflection:

Action

1.
2.
3.

The Monday Morning Fix

Positive Affirmation to Self

37. The Good You Do, Comes Back To You

I am reminded of a story of a woman who baked bread for members of her family and an extra one for hungry passer-by's. She kept the extra bread on the window-sill for whosoever would take it away. Every day, as the woman placed the bread on the sill, she offered a prayer for her son who had gone to a distant place to seek his fortune. Also, every single day, a hunchback came and took away the bread, instead of expressing gratitude he would mutter *"The evil you do remains with you. The good you do, comes back to you!"*

This went on, day after day. Every day the hunchback came, picked up the bread and uttered the words: *"The evil you do, remains with you. The good you do, comes back to you!"* The woman felt irritated. *"Not a word of gratitude"* she said to herself, *"Every day this hunchback utters this jingle. What does he mean?"*

One day, out of desperation, she decided to do away with him. *"I shall get rid of this hunchback"* she said. And what did she do? She added poison to the bread she prepared for him! As she was about to set it on the window sill, her hands trembled. *"What is this I am doing?"* she asked. Immediately, she threw the bread into the fire, prepared another one and put it on the window sill.

As usual, the hunchback came, picked up the bread and muttered *"The evil you do, remains with you. The good you do, comes back to you!"* Proceeding on his way, blissfully unaware of the war raging in the woman's mind.

For many months, there was no news of her son but she continued to pray for his safe return. That evening there was a knock on the door and as she opened it, she was surprised to see her son standing in the doorway. He was thin and lean. His garments, tattered and torn. He looked hungry, starved and weak and as he saw his mother, he said *"Mum, it is a miracle I am here. While I was but a mile away, I*

was so hungry that I collapsed. I would have died but an old hunchback passed by. I begged of him for a small part of his food and he was kind enough to give me a whole bread. As he gave it to me he said: 'This is what I eat every day, today I shall give it to you, your need is greater than mine.' "

As his mother listened, her face turned pale and she leaned against the door for support. She remembered the poisoned bread she had made that morning. Had she not burnt it, it would have been eaten by her own son and he would have lost his life! It was then that she realised the significance of the hunchback's words: *"The evil you do remains with you. The good you do, comes back to you!"*

Do good and do not ever stop doing good, even if it is not appreciated at that time.

The Monday Morning Fix

Reflection:

_____
_____
_____
_____
_____
_____
_____
_____
_____
_____
_____

Action

1.

2.

3.

Tony Henry

Positive Affirmation to Self

38. Mind Over Matter

How many of you believe that the way you think, impacts on how you feel?

That your thoughts create your reality?

How many of you woke up this morning and consciously created a future?

The biggest reason why most people do not do it is because they do not believe it is true or possible. If you knew and believed your thoughts created your destiny from a gut level, would you ever miss a day? And would you let any thought slip by your awareness that you did not want to experience?

Psychology Today suggests that the average person has between 50,000-70,000 thoughts per day. This breaks down to between 35-48 thoughts per minute. Of which approximately 90% of those thoughts are the same thoughts as the day before.

So, we can conclude that the same thoughts will lead to the same choices, the same choices will always create the same behaviours, the same behaviours will produce the same experiences and the same experiences will create the same emotions. The same emotions and feelings will drive the same exact thoughts!

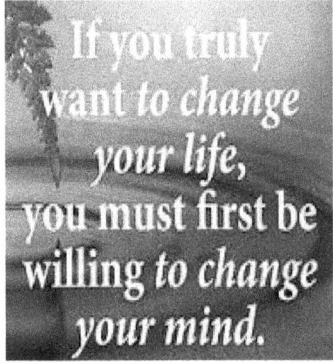

Therefore, would it not make sense to become more aware of what you think and in so doing you can change your thoughts, change your mind and change your life.

The Monday Morning Fix

Reflection:

_____
_____
_____
_____
_____
_____
_____
_____
_____
_____
_____

Action

1.

2.

3.

Tony Henry

Positive Affirmation to Self

39. Love...I Am Enough

What is love?...

Enter a room filled with people and ask the question, *"What is love?"* Do not be surprised at the variety of answers in reply. **LOVE** that four letter word bamboozles the best of us. Yet, we must **LOVE the good in us as it shines through and through.** Love begins with you. How you see yourself, how you treat yourself and how you express yourself, is a direct reflection of your understanding of yourself and your self-love. We are all born fully loaded with the concept of love, however, our environment, family and interactions both positive and negative, cause us to reject our very nature which is love.

Left unchecked you relegate yourself to a life of lack and discontentment, attracting all you say you do not want. Checked, love is cooperative, harmonising, accepting, forgiving, the essence of your soul, attracting abundance, healing, compassion, growth, trust, selflessness and respect. You are born of love therefore you are enough. You are strong enough to carry life's load on your shoulders, vulnerable enough to ask for help when you stumble and humble enough to admit the mistakes you have made. Yet, confident enough to laugh at yourself on either good or bad days, and human enough to take and give it your all.

You. Are. Enough. Let me repeat that so it goes through. You. Are. Enough.

Starting from today, acknowledge the fact that you are enough, that you are special, there is no one else like you and the world would not be same without you.

Right now, in this moment I am going to do what I can, with what I have and what I know, from where I am and that is enough!

Reflection:

Action

1.

2.

3.

Positive Affirmation to Self

40. It's Not Over Till It's Over

I am reminded of a time as a school leaver I thought I would never get a job. I would say that I went for hundreds of interviews all to no avail. When I got my all-important break, my worst nightmare began to unfold.... You see I got stuck in a lift as an adolescent and spent the next few years convincing everyone that the reason, I always used the stairs was because I was aiming to keep fit. The job that was advertised was for an electrical technician, what it failed to mention was that the role would be with a lift company. At that moment I thought my world had ended, it was not until the training officer convinced me that I would be fully trained to work on every aspect of the industry that I was able to relax. Often times in life, just when we make a decision to change for the better, we are reminded of all of our past failures, mistakes and flaws. So, we feel incapable of accomplishing anything worthwhile as we wrestle with the words, feelings and emotions of what

> **The temptation to quit will be greatest just before you are about to succeed.**

did not happen, what we failed to achieve, allowing the fear of failure to sabotage our opportunity for success.

Let's keep it real, anything worthwhile in life will come at a price. Yes, it may hurt, it may take time and it will require dedication. It will require willpower to make healthy decisions or sacrifices. You will need to push your mind and body to another level and even then, there will be temptation. However, in the end, it will be worth it.

So, before you think of quitting, remind yourself of why you started, why you felt the need for change and how your life and the lives of others will change for the greater good. Adopt a *'can do'* attitude, believe that you will receive and that you are enough. Do not allow your age, sex or skin colour to hold you back.

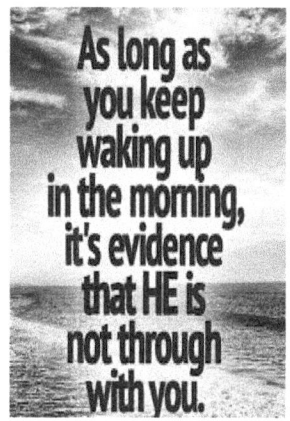

As long as you keep waking up in the morning, it's evidence that HE is not through with you.

Remember life is full of disappointments, failures and setbacks. None of these things can permanently stop you. You have the power in you to overcome anything that life throws at you. There is nothing as powerful as a made-up mind. Do not give up, cave in, or stop believing that it is possible. *It is not over until it is over.*

Reflection:

_____
_____
_____
_____
_____
_____
_____
_____
_____
_____
_____
_____

Action

1.

2.

3.

Positive Affirmation to Self

41. Echo

I am reminded of a story where a man and his son were walking in the forest. Suddenly the boy tripped and feeling a sharp pain, he screams, *"AHHHH!"* Surprised, he hears a voice coming from the mountain, *"AHHHH!"*

Filled with curiosity, he screams *"Who are you?"* but the only answer he receives is *"Who are you?"*, this makes him angry, so he shouts *"You're a coward!"* and the voice answers *"You're a coward!"* He looks at his father and asks, *"Dad what is going on?"*….

"Son," the man replies, *"pay attention."* Then he screams, *"I admire you!"* The voice answers *"I admire you!"* The father shouts again, *"You're wonderful!"* and the voice answers *"You're wonderful!"*

This rule of nature applies to every aspect of our lives. Life always gives you back what you give out. Your life is not a

The Monday Morning Fix

coincidence but a mirror of your own doing. Choose your
ECHO!

Reflection:

_____
_____
_____
_____
_____
_____
_____
_____
_____
_____

_____

Action

1.

2.

3.

Positive Affirmation to Self

42. Tapping Into Your Power

I am reminded of the time of my first boxing bout. I was drawn against someone who was older and I felt, better than me. However, my coach was of a very different opinion. The instructions were simple I had height and a reach advantage and all I needed to do was work my jab and wait for my opponent to navigate around it and then fire my right. 30 seconds into the fight an opportunity presented itself, I fired my right and bloodied my opponents' nose. Panic set in, was he going to go ballistic? Looking back at my corner I was advised more of the same, so said so done and a decisive victory for yours truly.

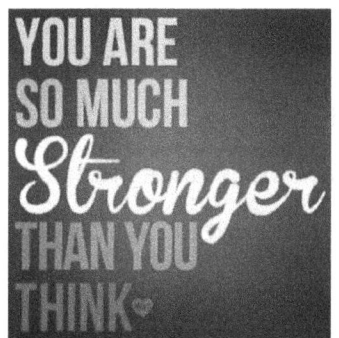

Each one of us, on some level, has tried elevating ourselves to a greater height or even a better way of living. Unfortunately, that is where we fail to achieve what we say we want - *"We Tried"* - but we did not really believe. The power is and has always been right where we are. The power is the essence of all that is good, it is divine and it operates in all of us, truth be told it is our birth right. When we make the shift and truly believe in the power that is within, we allow it to bring into our lives the very things we struggle with, not some things but all things. It is in our health, relationships, finances, state of mind and being. The power is the living force operating within us, buried beneath our ego, pride, personality, perceptions, fears and doubts. Be warned, whenever we make a stand to do that which is good and beneficial for us, there is often resistance from within. Resistance in the form of that little voice which will try reminding us about all the reasons why we cannot connect with our power and why it will work for everyone else but not for us.

This is the point where we have to affirm that: *"Divine love now dissolves and dissipates every wrong condition in our mind, body and affairs. Divine love is the most powerful chemical in the universe and dissolves everything which is not of itself."*

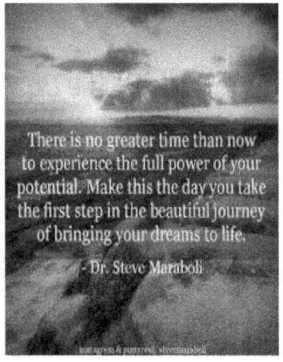

Reflection:

_____
_____
_____
_____
_____
_____
_____
_____
_____
_____
_____

Action

1.

2.

3.

Positive Affirmation to Self

43. Finish The Year Strong

As we rapidly approach the end of the year, it is my wish that you all **Finish the Year Strong.** Whether that be family coming together for an event, relationship having more quality time, work getting that promotion, business increasing the profit margin, health losing those extra pounds and pleasure going on that long overdue vacation. In order for you to **Finish Strong**, you might want to consider the following:

i'm not telling you it is going to be easy, i'm telling you it's going to be worth it.

1. Creating a success environment for yourself that produces consistent results.

2. Imposing strict deadlines on yourself and being ruthless about wasting time.

3. Hold yourself accountable, hour by hour.

4. Execute your plans like your life, career and future depended on it.

Every great life, career or family is run by someone with impeccably high standards, someone who is unwilling to negotiate with neither excuses nor mediocrity. The parent who works their 9-5 then comes home and works on their 5-9 side hustle.

What do we do now?

- Get Serious…set clear goals, step up your game, take no prisoners.
- Refuse to give up…winners never quit and quitters never win. Adopt a setback is a setup for a comeback mentality.
- Do things differently or do different things. Institute a few degrees of change and focus on what is been done well and ramp it up.

- Accelerate what you do and how you do it…more haste, less speed, develop a sense of urgency around all that you do with the end in mind. Visualise your desired outcome with all the benefits that come with successfully finishing the year strong.

- Be Relentless...means being unstoppable no matter what comes your way.

The Monday Morning Fix

Reflection:

_____
_____
_____
_____
_____
_____
_____
_____
_____
_____
_____

Action

1.

2.

3.

Tony Henry

Positive Affirmation to Self

44. What Do You Make?
(A Teacher's Perspective)

I am reminded of a story about a question posed to a teacher at a dinner party.

"What do you make?" Now for many of us this might have been a bit challenging, however I admit, I just love the way in which this particular teacher chose to respond. It is a lesson for us all.

"You want to know what I make? I make kids work harder than they ever thought they could. I can make a C+ feel like a Medal of Honour and an A- feel like a slap in the face."

"How dare you waste my time with anything less than your very best." I make kids sit through forty minutes of study time in absolute silence. *"No, you may not work in groups. No, you may not ask a question. Why I will not let you go to the bathroom? Because you are bored. And you do not really have to go to the bathroom, do you?"* I make parents tremble in fear when I call home *"Hi, this is Mr Mali, I hope I've not called at a bad*

time, I just wanted to talk to you about something your son said today to the biggest bully in the grade. He said, 'Leave the kid alone, I still cry sometimes, don't you? It's no big deal' "

And that was the noblest act of courage I have ever seen. I make parents see their children for who they are and what they can be. You want to know what I make? I make kids wonder, I make them question. I make them criticise. I make them apologise and mean it. I make them write. I make them read, read, read. I make them spell *'definitely beautiful, definitely beautiful, definitely beautiful'* over and over and over again until they never misspell either one of those words again. I make them show all their work in math and hide it on their final drafts in English. I make them understand that if you have got *this*, then you follow *this*, and if someone ever tries to judge you by what you make, you give them *this*. Here, let me break it down for you, so you know what I say is true: *"Teachers make a goddamn difference! Now what about you?"*

Success isn't about how much money you make, it's about the difference you make in people's lives.

The Monday Morning Fix

Reflection:

_____
_____
_____
_____
_____
_____
_____
_____
_____
_____
_____

Action

1.

2.

3.

Tony Henry

Positive Affirmation to Self

45. Three Types Of People

People do the strangest things. The next time you're challenged by the actions of a family member, partner, friend or co-worker use this breakdown of people to stay focused and true to yourself. Three types of people:

1. LEAF PEOPLE

Some people come into your life and they are like leaves on 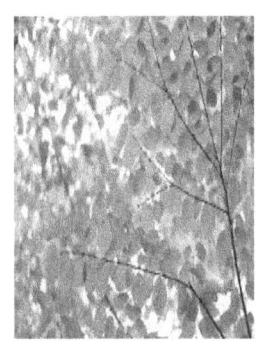 a tree - there for only a season. You cannot depend or count on them because they tend to be weak, only there to give you shade. Like leaves, they take what they need and as soon as it is cold or a strong wind blows in your life, they are gone. You cannot be angry at them it is just who they are.

2. BRANCH PEOPLE

There are those people who come into your life like branches on a tree. Stronger than leaves, you have to be careful with them. They will stick around through most seasons but if you go through a storm or two it is possible you could lose them. Most times they will break away when the going gets tough. So, you need to test them before you put all your weight onto them. In most cases they cannot handle too much but again, you cannot be mad with them, it is just who they are.

3. ROOT PEOPLE

If you can find some people in your life like the roots of a tree, then you have found something special. Like roots, they are hard to find because they are not trying to be seen. Their only job is to hold you up and help you live a strong and healthy life. If you thrive, they are happy. They stay low key and do not let the world know that they are there. And if you go through an awful storm, they will hold you up, nourish, feed and water you, come what may. Just as a tree has many limbs and many leaves, there are fewer roots. Look at your own life. How many leaves, branches and roots do you have? Who are you in other people's lives? **One day everything will make perfect sense, so for now, laugh at the confusion, smile through the tears, and**

keep reminding yourself that everything happens for a reason.

Reflection:

_____
_____
_____
_____
_____
_____
_____
_____
_____
_____
_____
_____

Action

1.

2.

3.

Positive Affirmation to Self

46. Making Sense Out Of Modern Day Nonsense

Recently I came across T. Harv Eker's *11 Principles To Activate Your Millionaire Mind*^{TM} and felt compelled to share. In a time and space where many people struggle to understand the money game, the 11 Principles gives all those who are prepared to shift gears and change their mindset, an opportunity to negotiate the benefits and challenges for a better financial future.

1. The universe gives you what you can handle
'Money miracles will occur once you demonstrate to the universe that you can handle your finances properly.'

2. No pain, no gain (at least at the beginning, if you are smart)
'If you are willing to do only what is easy. Life will be hard. But if you are willing to do what is hard, life will be easy'

3. If you are not growing, you are automatically dying
'If you are not doing as well as you would like, all that means is there is something you do not know.'

4. Clarity is Power

'The number one reason most people do not get what they want is that they do not know what they want.'

5. Gain wealth through purpose, contribution and successful people

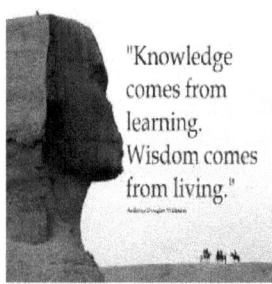

*'If your motivation for acquiring money or success comes from a non-supportive root such as fear, anger, or the need to "**PROVE**" yourself, your money will never bring you happiness.'*

6. Learn from other rich and successful people

'Rich people play the money game to win. Poor people play the money game not to lose.'

7. What you focus on expands

'Your field of focus determines what you find in life.'

8. Make a lot of money and help a lot of people

'The goal of truly rich people is to have massive wealth and for many of them, it is to help a lot of people.'

9. When you change your mindset, you will change your life

'It is not enough to be in the right place at the right time. You have to be the right person in the right place at the right time.'

10. Rich people are willing to do what average people will not

'Are you willing to work 16 hours a day? Rich people are. Are you willing to work seven days a week and sometimes most of your weekends? Rich people are.'

> "Lessons in life will be repeated until they are learned."

11. Know what it takes, do what it takes, never give up and focus, focus, focus

> *"Getting rich takes focus, courage, knowledge, expertise, 100 percent of your effort, a never give up attitude and of course a rich mindset."*
> **T. Harv Eker**

The Monday Morning Fix

Reflection:

_____

_____

_____

_____

_____

_____

_____

_____

_____

Action

1.

2.

3.

Positive Affirmation to Self

47. Your Health Is Your Wealth

(When was your last MOT)

It has been said that your Health is your Wealth, yet so 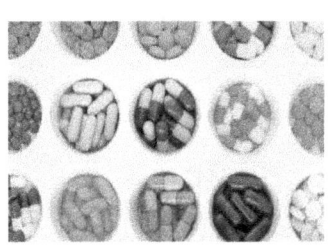 many people spend their health gaining wealth and then have to spend their wealth to regain their health. Many of us are car owners or know someone who owns a car, and in spite of the advancements in technology our modern-day cars still need to go into a garage for a **MOT** annually (Ministry of Transport, is an annual test of vehicle safety, roadworthiness aspects and exhaust emissions required in the UK). So, whether you are a human or a car, we all need to go in for a **MOT** in order to ensure our road worthiness.

Ignorance in this department often begins with a minor hiccup in the balance between our mental, physical and spiritual equilibrium. With the introduction and taking of the vast array of energy boosting drinks, tablets and potions, many ignore the warning signs and continue to punish their body (temple), to operate under more and more unnatural and stressful conditions.

But what happens when our physical bodies show no visible signs of wear and tear, yet internally we become unsettled with our sense of well-being? What we once took for granted, like getting a full night's sleep, waking up in the morning with a spring in our stride, doing a full day's work with fuel enough left in the tank for a night out, becomes a distant memory for all the wrong reasons.

It is at this point, we all need to take stock, asking the question *"When Was My Last MOT?"* In a day and an age when it is all too easy to put our overall health and well-being on the back burner for the sake of our jobs, careers, business and families, I truly believe we need to take stock of what a balanced and fruitful life looks and feels like. A life with little to no stress, minimal ailments, guilt free vacations or ample quality time with family and friends.

Your **MOT** is personal to you and by adopting the following recommendations I believe you have a great opportunity to do something your future self would thank you for:

1. When you wake in the morning, spend some time designing the day how you would like to experience it.

2. Drink a glass of water, your body will thank you for it.

3. Based on your personal beliefs make time for prayer, meditation and or mindfulness.

4. Introduce some form of physical activity into your life - exercise, walk or run do something.

5. Your body is a temple, it is where you live. Treat it like you would treat a treasured possession. Eat things that are good for you.

6. Invest in yourself. In the words of Ray Kroc *"When you are green your growing, when you are ripe you rot."*

7. Adapt an attitude of gratitude in all things, take nothing for granted.

8. *"Be the change you want to see"* - Ghandi

9. Walk in love, be love.

10. Give freely of your time, money, gifts, talents, abilities.

Always remember that your health is your wealth.

The Monday Morning Fix

Reflection:

_____
_____
_____
_____
_____
_____
_____
_____
_____
_____
_____

Action

1.

2.

3.

Tony Henry

Positive Affirmation to Self

48. The Giving Tree

I am reminded of the Shel Silverstein classic, *The Giving Tree,* which I felt compelled to share with you.

Once there was a tree....and she loved a little boy. Every 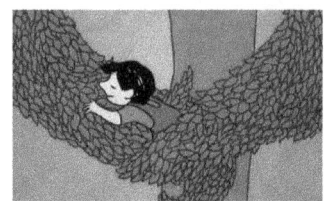 day, the boy came and gathered her leaves, making them into crowns and playing king of the forest. He would climb up her trunk, swing from her branches, eat apples and when he was tired, sleep in her shade. The tree was happy but as time went by, the boy grew older and the tree was often alone. Then one day the boy returned and the tree said, *"Come, Boy, come and climb up my trunk and swing from my branches and eat apples and play in my shade and be happy."*

"I'm too big to climb and play" said the boy. *"I want to buy things and have fun. I want some money?"*

"I'm sorry" said the tree, *"but I have no money. I only have leaves and apples. Take my apples

Boy, and sell them in the city. Then you will have money and you will be happy." And so, the boy climbed the tree, gathered her apples and carried them away, and the tree was happy.

This time, the boy stayed away for longer....and the tree was sad. Then one day the boy came back and the tree shook with joy and said *"Come Boy, climb my trunk and swing from my branches and be happy."*

"I'm too busy to climb trees" said the boy. *"I want a house to keep me warm"* he said. *"I want a wife and I want children, and so I need a house. Can you give me a house?"*

"I have no house" said the tree. *"The forest is my house but you may cut off my branches and build a house. Then you will be happy."* And so, the boy cut off her branches and carried them away to build his house, and the tree was happy. This time the boy stayed away much longer than previously.

When he returned, the tree was so happy she could hardly speak. *"Come Boy"* she whispered *"come and play."*

"I'm too old and sad to play" said the boy. *"I want a boat that will take me far away from here. Can you give me a boat?"*

"Cut down my trunk and make a boat" said the tree. *"Then you can sail away and be happy."* And so, the boy cut down her trunk and made a boat and sailed away, and the tree was happy ...well not really.

After a very long time, the boy finally came back. *"I'm sorry Boy"* said the tree *"but I have nothing left to give you. My apples are gone."*

"My teeth are too weak for apples" said the boy.

"My branches are gone" said the tree. *"You cannot swing on them."*

"I'm too old to swing on branches" said the boy.

"My trunk is gone" said the tree. *"You cannot climb."*

"I'm too tired to climb" said the boy.

"I'm sorry" sighed the tree.

"I wish that I could give you something but I have nothing left. I'm just an old stump. I'm sorry."

"I don't need very much now" said the boy. *"Just a quiet place to sit and rest. I'm very tired."*

"Well" said the tree, straightening herself as much as she could, *"well, an old stump is good for sitting and resting come Boy, sit down. Sit down and rest."* And the boy did. And the tree was happy.

This classic has been interpreted in many ways, I'll leave you with this.

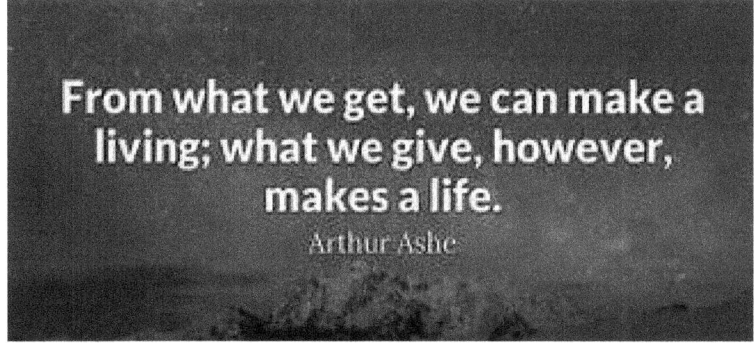

The Monday Morning Fix

Reflection:

_____
_____
_____
_____
_____
_____
_____
_____
_____
_____
_____

Action

1.

2.

3.

Tony Henry

Positive Affirmation to Self

49. Where Will You Be Five Years From Today?

Where Will You Be Five Years from Today? 260 Weeks, 1,825 Days, 2,333,000 Minutes. Put another way - where do you see yourself five years from now? Project Manager, Accountant, Lawyer, Property Investor, Teacher, Doctor or Nurse. The key question I ask is: *"Will you still be trading your time for money?"* or *"Will you be enjoying quality time with more than enough money?"*

It is your Time, it is your Life, what are you going to do with it? What could you do in five years? The answer depends on what you do today, tomorrow, next week, next month and all year. Five years is long enough to accomplish almost any goal you may have, however ambitious. Would you finally get around to writing your book, travelling the world or setting up your own business – secure in the knowledge that your retirement fund is no longer a problem, based on your financial forecast.

You can go on living how your living right now. No one is going to stop you from living a mediocre life. No one is going to come along and change your life for you. At some point you are going to have to acknowledge your blind spots and realise that if you continue to do what you have always done, you will get what you have always got. The only way you will be where you want in five years, is to start now - today. Today is the only period of time you have for you to change. It has been said *"A goal without a plan is just a wish"* and *"If your dream does not scare you it is not big enough."*

Another question commonly asked when looking to step out of your comfort zone and into your desired future is *'What is your **WHY?**'* I recently asked myself that very same question and my answer was:

"To spend more quality time with my family (children and grandchildren) when I want and to do what I want without having to worry about finances."

So, if you are anything like me and truly believe that there is more to life than just working to pay bills and dreading the Monday morning commute:

> ***"Don't count the days, make the day's count"***
> Muhammad Ali

The only place success comes before work is in the dictionary.

Reflection:

_____
_____
_____
_____
_____
_____
_____
_____
_____
_____
_____
_____

Action

1.

2.

3.

The Monday Morning Fix

Positive Affirmation to Self

50. Unique Different But Equal

Have you ever wondered what your life would be like, if you were to allow the authentic you the opportunity to play full out? Realising your unique combination of skills, talents, abilities, network of friends, acquaintances and opportunities. How would your life be if instead of playing small you allowed your unique gift to shine? Turning that hobby of occasionally writing for personal therapy to being a world-renowned author.

There is nothing more powerful than to recognise the power of individuality. There is nothing more powerful than to recognise that God made you an individual, a unique one of one of one on the entire earth. Irrespective of how many people exist in the world, there is only one **YOU!** The

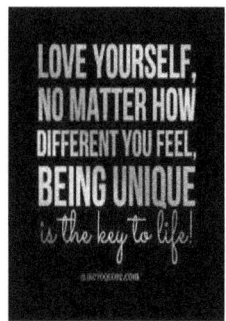

moment you recognise the power of your own individuality, it will be the start of something great. Do not allow your environment, your family or job to determine who you are or who you may become. Always remember you are one of one of one. There is something special about **YOU.**

You were not created to do the same, act the same or be the same as everyone else. You are **Unique**, **Different** but **Equal**. In order to make the world a better place, we all need to start looking for and appreciate the differences within each of us. We need to stop complaining, competing and comparing and start sharing, caring and embracing the fact we were born different to make a difference.

Unique Different But Equal

Reflection:

_____
_____
_____
_____
_____
_____
_____
_____
_____
_____
_____
_____

Action

1.

2.

3.

The Monday Morning Fix

Positive Affirmation to Self

51. Self-Awareness

Self-Awareness can be described as having a clear perception of your personality, including strengths, weaknesses, thoughts, beliefs, motivation, and emotions. Self-Awareness gives you a greater understanding of self, other people, how they perceive you, your attitude and your responses to them in any given moment or circumstance.

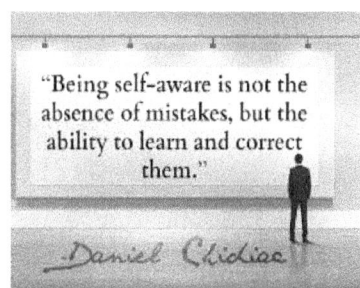

Being able to catch yourself when you realise that your thoughts, feelings or emotions are being counterproductive is an art worthy of mastery. And to the person who embarks on this journey and conquers the art of self-awareness the benefits, are mind blowing. Self-awareness is a key ingredient to success and to leading a prosperous life, if you have it, teach it, if you lack it, seek it.

4 Tips to enhance your Self-Awareness:

1. **Create some space for yourself.** Leave yourself some time and space every day – perhaps first thing

in the morning or half an hour before sleep when you stay away from the digital distractions and spend some time with yourself, reading, writing, meditating, and connecting with yourself.

2. **Keep a journal.** Numerous studies have shown that people that keep a journal are happier and more successful. The whole point of this exercise is to become more in tune of how you feel every day and then looking back and reflecting on it.

Wisdom tends to grow in proportion to one's awareness of one's ignorance.

Anthony de Mello

The value is not in the writing of itself but in the reading of it when you are in a different state of mind.

3. **Gain different perspectives.** Ask for feedback. In order to get a balanced assessment of where you truly are and how you are perceived, it is worth enlisting the help of family and friends who you respect and trust. Ask them what they think your

strengths and weaknesses are and let them know that they can be 100% honest with you.

4. **Always play to your strengths.** It is much easier to become a public speaker if you enjoy being the centre of attention and a bit of an extrovert. The point is, in life you are going to have certain predispositions to certain activities. This can be from birth or something you acquired throughout your life. Whatever the case may be, it is much easier to work on your strengths rather than to improve on your weaknesses.

The Monday Morning Fix

Reflection:

_____
_____
_____
_____
_____
_____
_____
_____
_____
_____
_____

Action

1.

2.

3.

Positive Affirmation to Self

52. The Value Of Life

A man went to a Guru and asked *"What is the value of life?"* The guru gave him one stone and said *"Find out the value of this stone, but don't sell it."*

The man took the stone to an Orange Seller and asked him for its worth. The Orange Seller saw the shiny stone and

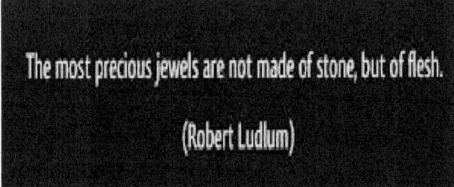
The most precious jewels are not made of stone, but of flesh.
(Robert Ludlum)

said *"You can take twelve oranges and give me the stone."* The man apologised and said that the Guru had asked him not to sell it. He went ahead and found a Vegetable Seller and asked *"What is the value of this stone?"*

The seller saw the shiny stone and said *"Take one sack of potatoes and give me the stone."* The man again apologised and said he could not sell it. Further ahead, he went into a Jewellery shop and asked the Jeweller the value of the stone. Looking under a lens, he said *"I'll give you £50.00 for this stone."* When the man shook his head, the Jeweller said *"Alright, alright, how about £500.00."* The man explained that he could not sell the stone.

Further ahead, the man saw a Precious Stones store and in there, he asked the seller the value of the stone. When the seller saw the big ruby, he took it and placed it on a red cloth. He then walked around it in circles, bending down and touching his head.

"From where did you get this priceless ruby?" he asked.

"Even if I sell the whole world and my life, I wouldn't be able to purchase this priceless stone." Stunned and confused, the man returned to the Guru and told him what had happened.

"Now tell me the value of life?" The Guru asked. *"The answers you got from the Orange Seller, the Vegetable Seller, the Jeweller and the Precious Stone seller, explain the value of life...You may be a precious stone,*

even priceless, but people will value you based on their financial status, their level of information, their belief in you, their motive behind entertaining you, their ambition, and their risk-taking ability. But do not fear, you will surely find someone who will discern your true value." Respect yourself.

Never sell yourself cheap.

You are rare, Unique, Original and the only one of your kind.

You are a masterpiece because you are MASTER'S PIECE.

Reflection:

Action

1.
2.
3.

Positive Affirmation to Self

Endorsements

"Tony is a special human being whose commitment to elevating humanity is second to none, as you will realise when you work your way through this book and apply the simple action steps each week." **Kalpesh Patel - Trained over 500,000 Entrepreneurs and Leaders, Top 60 International Speakers List, Top 50 Direct Sales Leaders Worldwide, International Podcast, TV, Radio, News & Web Interviews & Author**

"Hey Tony I am super impressed with your work here, it really is so much more than a book, it's a life workbook and contains so many gems for a reader to awaken to what is keeping them stuck. But more importantly your great work offers readers the opportunity to experience a powerful moment in every chapter every week for a year, leaving them with a more empowering perspective on their life.

The reflections, actions and affirmations in every chapter make this so much more than just a book, this is as I say, 'A Workbook for Living an Empowered Purposeful Life' and in the hands of someone committed to make the best of their life it offers a pathway to success that without the book they would find really difficult to uncover..." **Tony and Nikki Vee**

www.ingramcontent.com/pod-product-compliance
Lightning Source LLC
Chambersburg PA
CBHW060500090426
42735CB00011B/2061